the media st

iPad VIDEO PRODUCTION

Bob Gilmurray

MIGHTIER PEN PUBLISHING

ISBN: 1494306859
ISBN-13: 978-1494306854

CONTENTS

Introduction for tutors

This book is written for students enrolled on media production courses in schools and colleges which include modules in video production. It is particularly well suited to students in the UK who are taking BTEC Nationals and Higher Nationals, OCR Cambridge Technicals, and similar vocational media programmes.

While relevant aspects of media theory are introduced, and tasks are placed into their theoretical context, the main emphasis is upon the practical issues that arise when the student experiences - possibly for the first time - the challenge of working as a member of a team to plan and create an original video product, and they are being assessed on how well they do.

My starting point in writing this book was the realisation that the iPad has very rapidly become an essential and ubiquitous tool in education. Schools, particularly, are everywhere investing hugely in it, many giving or loaning all their students one each, which they take to all their classes. It replaces notebooks, ringbinders, and, to a large extent, computer suites; and it pays for itself in the saving on the photocopying budget. Worksheets can be uploaded to cloud storage by the tutor, and downloaded by the student. Students can hand in work in the same way. They can link interactively to the smart-board in the classroom; they can use it to draw pictures, take photographs, make audio and video recordings, make scientific and mathematical calculations, compose and arrange music, access the internet - and, of course, write an essay.

This is a huge investment for a school, and it is understandable that there will undoubtedly be, as a result, some reluctance on the part of school managers to spend even more money on specialist equipment that might no longer be necessary. "If it can be done on their iPad, then that's how they do it," is likely to increasingly become the budget-holder's mantra for the foreseeable future.

While there are still very strong arguments for using high-end specialist equipment on vocational programmes, especially at advanced levels, the iPad cannot simply be dismissed as 'toy technology'. It is capable of high quality HD video and sound; reliable apps have by now been developed for most production and post-production needs (except, so far, compositing); and peripherals are now widely available, most importantly tripod-mounting cradles, and interfaces for external microphones. As much of this is not yet common knowledge, I have devoted much of this book to suggestions and advice on equipment and apps.

Examination boards running vocational qualifications usually require that a centre's level of equipment and ICT resourcing should be appropriate to the industry. For the video industry, digital convergence and the increasing market-share of online forms of distribution have resulted in a blurring of the distinction between 'amateur' and 'professional' equipment. News and documentary footage is now sometimes produced on smartphones. Entire feature films are shot using video-capable DSLR stills cameras. It would be difficult, now, to come up with a strong reason why a combination of iPads for acquisition and desktop computers for editing should not satisfy these requirements, in general education, at all but the highest levels of programme.

There is a plethora of terminology in use for education providers: school, academy, college, and so on. For simplicity's sake, in this book I have chosen to refer to them all as 'colleges', and to students being 'at college'. This should be understood as generic. Similarly, I refer to academic staff as 'tutors'. For this, read 'teacher', 'lecturer', 'assessor', as appropriate to your situation.

1. On my iPad? – *really?*

If you are already using an iPad for most of your work in most of your classes, it makes absolute sense to use it for your video production assignments. It replaces a whole raft of expensive and complicated production and editing equipment, and also enables you to complete all your planning and pre-production work on the same device. It even gives you immediate access to public distribution channels for your finished product (such as YouTube and Vimeo) - something no traditional method of video production can offer.

However, there are significant limitations to what is, essentially, a point-and-shoot device. You will have to learn to work within these limitations, and adopt a rather different approach to acquisition than you would with a normal video camera. In doing this, though, you are likely to find that it will actually help you to make a better video - because it will prevent you from committing some of the basic errors that mar so many non-professional video productions. The most common of these are:

Zooming when what you really want is a cut. Zooming is an un-natural action (our eyes are not fitted with a zoom facility), so we notice it. A zoom calls attention to the presence of a camera. Usually, we want viewers to focus on the content of our film, not on the shooting technique. This is especially important in drama, where we want our audience engaged with the storyline and characters, not distracted by reminders that 'this is a film'. A cut, on the other hand, is more readily accepted by our brains as equivalent to our natural action in flicking our focus of attention around, sometimes homing in on detail, sometimes taking in the whole picture. Cuts are mostly invisible: we don't notice them; they are not intrusive in the way that zooms are. If you want to move from a mid-shot to a close-up, for example, do it at the editing stage with a cut; not by zooming in.

Worse is the tendency of the inexperienced camera-operator to zoom in and out for no particular reason. Often this is combined with panning around, also in an apparently random way. Usually this is either a misguided attempt to 'follow the action', or simply an itchy-fingered inability to leave camera controls alone.

Non-matching picture and sound. In a professionally-made film, the sound matches the picture. In wide-shot, voices sound distant: not just low in volume, but also with a high proportion of indirect to direct sound. Cut to close-up, and the sound is also close: both louder and more resonant. It is as though we are suddenly two feet away from the conversation, when, a second before, we were twenty feet away. The quality of the sound is at all times appropriate to the degree of distance between the viewer and the subject that the framing suggests.

In non-professional video productions using traditional cameras this is all too often not successfully achieved - or even attempted. The reason is usually that people get into the habit of using the zoom control to frame every shot. They stand wherever is convenient, and then zoom in or out to the framing they want. It's an understandable error - it is, after all, the main advantage the zoom control offers - but if your microphone is attached to your camera, the result will always be unsatisfactory sound. Some manufacturers claim to have overcome this problem with so-called 'zoom microphones', which alter their pick-up angle in relation to the zoom position of the lens, but the result is seldom wholly convincing. The only way properly to match sound to picture is to ensure that the microphone is placed at an appropriate distance for the framing of each shot. The easiest way to do this (and the *only* way, if you are using an onboard microphone) is to ignore the zoom control altogether, and move *yourself*, camera, microphone and all, into the required position for each shot.

The limitations of the iPad prevent you from committing these two cardinal errors, because *you can't zoom with an iPad**.

* well, strictly speaking, you sort-of can. Some apps, such as FiLMiC PRO, offer digital zoom. Don't use it - at least, not for zooming: it's really, really rubbish. Digital zoom works by selecting and then enlarging the central portion of the existing image. It does this by reducing the pixel resolution of the image. The more 'zoomed-in' you are, the more pixillated the image becomes. In very bright lighting, you might just get away with a small amount of zoom. In anything less than bright light, the degradation of the image will be obvious. Think of digital zoom as a special effect - for instance if your script calls for footage from a security camera, or you want to create a 'Blair Witch' type sequence. For everything else, just accept that you can't zoom: if you want a close-up, you have to physically move in closer. The result will be a more natural-looking close-up, which doesn't suffer from the foreshortening effect of a telephoto lens; plus, if you are using a microphone attached to the iPad, you will be rewarded with great sound, instantly making your production more professional.

2. Equipment

Things you need

There are three accessories that you absolutely can't do without: firstly, *a bracket or cradle* that enables you to attach your iPad to a tripod. Shooting hand-held with an iPad feels very awkward: its shape is all wrong for the purpose, plus the lens is mounted off-centre. The result is usually unacceptably wobbly footage.

There are a number of such devices readily available on the internet, ranging from simple clamps to expensive housings that enable you to attach supplementary lenses, rifle microphones, and LED video lights. I would advise going for a basic one: the tripod bush is the only thing you really need. Mounting to a tripod gives you stability, and also enables you to execute smooth pans. If you find them a bit of an encumbrance, try using a monopod instead: they will give you sufficient stability for a steady shot, while also being a lot quicker to move around.

Secondly, you'll need *an external microphone* of some kind. The onboard microphone is mono, and of acceptable, but not great, quality. This would not be a major concern if it was effectively insulated from the rest of the casing. Unfortunately, it isn't - so it picks up handling noise loud and clear. Even mounted to a tripod, any movements in-shot are likely to be noisy. It's necessary, therefore, to find an alternative way of recording sound. The possibilities are:

> • Attach an external microphone to the headphone socket. This isn't quite as straightforward as it sounds, because the socket isn't a normal stereo jack socket, so you will need a converter lead. An ideal solution is the iRig Pre Microphone Interface, which gives you an XLR input, a pre-amp, 48V phantom power (for condenser microphones) if you need it, and a headphone-thru socket, all in one neat little box. This arrangement will give you a significant improvement in sound - though it will still be in mono.

iRig Pre

• Attach an external USB microphone to the dock connector via the USB adaptor. This will give you high-quality sound (in stereo, if you use a stereo microphone). The downside is that the dock connector (whether 30-pin or the 8-pin Lightning connector) isn't built to have heavy peripherals hanging from it, and you really don't want to risk damaging the socket (if you do, you won't be able either to re-charge its battery, or run it off the mains supply; it'll be a dead iPad. You have been warned…).

• Record all your sound separately. You could, for instance, use another iPad, set up with an audio recording app (such as iTalk Recorder, or Voice Recorder HD), or you could use one or more iPhones (with similar apps), hidden around the set, or in your presenter's/talent's top pocket. Best of all, if you have access to one, you could use a digital audio recorder such as the Zoom H4n, which will record in stereo or multi-track, and has both its own microphones and input sockets for external microphones. Whichever, if you take this approach, you will need to use the clapperboard technique for all acquisition (if you don't have a clapperboard, just get someone to hold up an ID card for each shot - e.g. 'Scene 3, shot 1, take 2' - then clap their hands, so that there is a peak on the audio waveform you can use at the editing stage to line the sound up with the picture). Although this may seem quite complicated, it's the approach I would recommend: it gives you the most freedom to work creatively with your soundtrack in post-production; and it's the one that most closely replicates professional practice.

Thirdly, unless you are shooting entirely indoors, you will need *some kind of hood* to enable you to see the iPad screen while you are shooting. Bright as the iPad screen is, it can't compete with sunlight; and you can't film if you can't see what you're filming. There's a clever solution just on the market (as I write) in the USA called The Hoodi (www.hoodivision.com): it's a folding cloth hood which attaches to the iPad with magnets. It should be available in the UK sometime soon. Failing this, a black golf umbrella held by an assistant usually works quite well - or if you prefer to be more independent, a clamp-on telescopic sun-umbrella, which you can easily clip onto your tripod.

Things you don't need

Telephoto supplementary lenses. These don't give you anything you couldn't achieve better by simply moving to a different position; plus they may cause fringing or vignetting. The only additional lenses I would consider are a close-up or macro lens, if I was intending to make a video about insects, or a wide-angle lens if I wanted to shoot in wide-screen 'Cinerama'. If you want to use additional lenses, you will need a specialist iPad cradle, such as the Makayama Movie Mount, which has a sliding mount for 37mm lenses*.

*A word of caution, though: the screw thread on this lens mount is plastic, and easily damaged. I have customized mine by permanently glueing in a 37mm UV filter. This gives me a metal front-thread for attaching additional supplementary lenses and filters.

Coloured Filters. If you want, for instance, to give your footage an un-natural tint, it's better to make the adjustments at the editing stage, with a grading app (see Post-production), rather than by shooting through stage lighting gel, or whatever (if you do decide to use filters, remember to set your white-balance *before* attaching the filter).

Onboard video lights. An LED video light mounted onto an iPad cradle will give you harsh, flat, shadowless illumination. If you want a shot of a rabbit trapped in headlights, that's fine. Otherwise, if you need to brighten the scene, do it from the sides, not the front (with proper lights, such as redheads, if your college has them).

Video recording apps

The iPad comes with the ability to record video with its *Camera* app. Just switch it to video, rather than still image. It's fine: so long as you're using just the one iPad, and scenes in natural light don't take long to shoot, its only significant limitation is that it only has one button to lock both exposure and focus. It's a grid-shaped button that appears briefly on the screen when you tap the key point of interest. This determines both the overall exposure level and the point of sharpest focus of your image (if the result is unsatisfactory, just tap the screen again somewhere else). If you tap and hold, focus and exposure will be locked (an 'AE lock' flag appears), enabling you to re-frame the shot at that setting before tapping the record button.

You'll need to use AE lock if your shot includes any camera movement such as a pan. If you don't, the iris will open up or close down as you move between brighter and darker areas of the scene, which looks very amateur. Your decision in selecting your key point of interest will depend on your creative intention: for instance, you might not want average exposure; you might prefer to shoot high key or low key. If so, you may have to select an area of the screen that is not, in fact, your key point of interest, in order to get the exposure the way you want it. This area will then also become the area of sharpest focus – meaning that your *actual* key point of interest may be slightly soft. Bearing this in mind, if you are happy to do without a separate means of focusing your shot as you want it, then Camera* may be all you need.

 note: if you are using the iMovie app on your iPad for your editing, you can film within iMovie: selecting the camera icon in iMovie simply launches the Camera app.

If, however, you're planning to edit together footage from a multi-iPad shoot, or you are shooting parts of the same scene at different times of day, then Camera's absence of manual control over white balance may become an issue. You may be able to correct this at the editing stage if you have a grading app, but it's better not to have the problem in the first place.

If you need this additional control over composition and white balance (or you really, really want to use digital zoom), then *FiLMiC PRO* is the app to go for. It gives you separate slide-y lock buttons for focus and exposure plus a white balance lock, digital zoom with three programmable presets, audio metering, a histogram, a choice of aspect ratios, and a choice of screen resolutions, frame rates, and bit-rates. Its clip preview screen also allows you to trim clips before export.

FiLMiC Pro

Video editing apps

Video editing on the iPad means *iMovie*, yes? Well, probably yes. It's easy to learn, easy to use, and gives you all the basic facilities you are likely to want most of the time. It's not Final Cut Pro - but then, nothing running on an iPad ever will be. The main limitation is that it only has one video timeline, so you can't do 'green screen' (or any other form of compositing or digital effects work).* However, it does allow you to build up multiple audio tracks, so you can edit and mix dialogue, sound effects and music as separate elements, plus you can edit the in and out points of your audio separately from the video transition point, to create 'J or L cuts' (sound starting before or stopping after the associated picture at a scene change). The current update (version 2.0) also offers a picture-in-picture facility. There are a few minor irritations: the default transition is a crossfade - you have to select a straight cut, if that's what you want - and the 'themes' approach to graphics and titling is a bit cheesy, unless you take the trouble to customise it.

actually there are a few small developers and open source projects working on this, so things might change in the future. At the moment, though, there's nothing available I would take seriously. If you want to do compositing, stick with After Effects or Final Cut Pro on a desktop computer.

If you're looking for an alternative to iMovie while sticking with the iPad, the best is *Pinnacle Studio*. It looks quite similar to iMovie, except that there is an additional strip of thumbnail images of your clips above the timeline, making it easy to drag and drop clips to the timeline, while retaining an overview of the whole project. There's still only one video timeline, though, so you can't do compositing; but it does provide what it calls 'montage clips' - drop-zone templates for basic picture-in-picture effects. On the other hand, there's no provision on the audio tracks for J or L cuts.

Both apps are great for basic editing. You'll have to export your footage at least to full iMovie on a laptop, however, if you want access to tools such as layered video effects. If your college is set up with Final Cut or Adobe Premiere/After Effects on desktop PC's, then that's obviously the way to go for advanced editing work - though expect the learning curve to be quite steep.

Lighting
General

The use of additional lighting can improve your shots in a number of different ways. However, you have to balance against this the general inconvenience of transporting and setting up lamps, and the extra health and safety implications this will impose. You can't travel light and shoot quickly if you're taking a flight-case full of blondes.

Consider using additional lighting in the following types of situation:

- It's going to be too dark to film otherwise;

- You want to create modelling on faces, or more directional light generally;

- You will be shooting for hours, and you know that you will have continuity problems if you rely solely on the ambient lighting. which will change throughout the day;

- You want to create low-key mood lighting (indoors);

- You want to create a lighting effect (such as uplighting faces, or creating fantasy sequences);

- You want to warm up the natural daylight (outdoors).*

as in The Darling Buds of May television series, which created a nostalgic and romantic look through the use of gold/pink additional lighting. You'll find you can achieve this satisfactorily outdoors with portable lamps, provided you don't shoot wider than mid-shot.

If you simply want to set up professional-looking balanced lighting for, say, an interview for a documentary, then the standard set-up is called '3-point lighting'.

This uses three lamps: a key light, a fill light, and a back light. The key light is normally placed quite high, and at around 45° to the subject. The fill light is less bright, placed on the opposite diagonal, normally lower down, and softened with a frost filter. The back light is also less bright and softer than the key light, and placed behind the subject to create three-dimensional modelling and separation from the back wall. If you want both interviewer and interviewee lit, then you have the choice of either using more lamps, or utilising one person's key light as the other person's back light (over the shoulder), with the fill placed front-on covering both subjects.

There are many variations on this theme, which would by themselves fill another book. If you want to know more, there are plenty of handbooks and internet tutorial videos on the subject. Go do some research...

Day-for-night

Some film genres - notably horror and thriller - demand night shooting. The atmosphere of such films depends on it. They are made to be tense and scary, and they succeed largely through playing upon our fear of the dark. However, this poses practical problems for the film-maker. For one thing, it's unsocial hours, and very inconvenient for everyone involved. Nobody wants to be out shooting at three in the morning. For another, it's hard to film in low-light conditions, even with professional cameras. With an iPad, it's impossible. No light: no movie.

The solution is to shoot during the daytime, and process your shots to make it look like night. You can do this in one of two ways. The easy way (and the best and most reliable way) is to do it at the editing stage, using your grading app to adjust the brightness and contrast, and apply a dark blue tint. However, if you want to have a bit of fun, you could try doing it the traditional way, at the shooting stage. White-balance your iPad on a yellow card (which tips the colour rendition towards blue); then, if you can, attach a neutral density filter (such as an ND4) in front of the lens to reduce the incoming light level and depth-of-field.

Either way, it's best to avoid having expanses of sky in your shots, as in daylight the sky is brighter than the scene below, whereas at night it is darker. Also, if you want shots of brightly-lit windows in houses, then it's best to shoot at dusk, rather than in full daylight. Shoot into the sun when you are filming people: that way they are back-lit, and will be in semi-silhouette, which looks more natural in a night-time scene than being able to see their faces clearly.

Film Noir

If you want to shoot a film in the style of German Expressionism (*The Cabinet of Dr Calgari*, *Nosferatu*) or the later American neo-expressionist style Film Noir (*The*

Big Sleep, *The Maltese Falcon*), then you need to think in terms of:

- Unbalanced composition (disturbing, un-natural camera-angles);

- Black-and-white;

- Low key, high contrast lighting (blocks or pools of bright light and deep shadow).

The iPad will film in colour. You then make your footage black-and-white at the editing stage, with your grading app. Everything else you have to achieve at the shooting stage, with the use of hard, narrow-beam spotlighting and careful adjustment of masks, gobos or barn doors. You need, at the very least, redheads. Blondes are better, because they are higher wattage. Best of all is proper stage lighting (profile spotlights, which, with the use of masks behind the lens, can give you a hard, straight-edged beam, plus, with gobos, lighting effects such as the shadow of a venetian blind on a wall).

For this very important reason, the best place to shoot this kind of film is not on location; it is in a theatre, auditorium or film/video studio - somewhere that is equipped with a proper lighting rig. Forget filming in an office: instead, create an office set in a studio, or on a stage.

3: Group-work issues

Video production assignments require you to work in small teams. This is partly for practical reasons: there are very few types of video production you can realistically achieve on your own (animation, perhaps; maybe the video diary), and partly because this is how it is done in the industry. On vocational courses, you learn skills for employment, so the approach you are taught is the professional one.

Working with others is a skill in itself, and a very important one to develop for all sorts of careers. Whatever you may think, it doesn't just come naturally. Most video projects that fail, fail because the group is dysfunctional. The individuals don't bond as a team, don't pull together, argue all the time. Their relationships to each other are competitive and selfish, when they should be co-operative and team-building; and so, inevitably, the project falls apart in a mess of demotivated rancour.

The most frequent distress-cry heard by tutors in the early stages of a video production assignment is: "Please can I just work on my own? *Why* can't I work on my own? I could do so much better work if I was allowed to work on my own. On my own, I could get a Distinction. If I have to work with X, Y, and Z, I'll probably just get a Pass. It'll pull down my grade. It's not fair!"

Sorry - the answer's "No". It's understandable that students often feel this way - for all the reasons I'm about to list below. You're just going to have to accept, though, that (a) it's impractical; and (b) your marks aren't coming just from the quality of the video product you produce - they're coming from the quality of the video product you produce *and* the quality of your contribution to the production process. You can't hold a planning meeting on your own, or show how good a team member or delegator you are. Your ability to work together with others is an important part of what is being assessed.

Here are some issues that frequently get in the way of successful group work. Whether you recognise or identify with any of them or not, it's worth discussing these issues openly together in your group, in the early stages of a project. If you can identify potential pitfalls early on, and come to an amicable agreement on the strengths and weaknesses of the group *as a group*, then you've made a good start on being able to deal with them before they become a major problem.

• Wanting only to work with your friends. Finding it difficult to establish a working relationship with people you aren't close to on a personal level.

• Being too wedded to your own ideas. Wanting only to work on your own idea; losing interest if the group decide against your idea. Objecting to having your initial idea developed in another direction by others. Not wanting to work collaboratively. Not taking an interest in other people's ideas.

• Being negative: quick to criticise others' ideas, but slow to suggest ideas of your own or positive ways forward. Being too ready to turn a discussion into an argument, not seeing how destructive this might be to group cohesion - and to progress.

• Wanting either to do everything yourself, or order everyone else around. Being the over-pushy 'group leader' who either doesn't allow anyone else to contribute anything important, or treats the other members of the group as servants, rather than fellow-collaborators.

• Being shy and retiring, letting others take the lead in meetings and decision-making. Ending up assisting, instead of fully participating. Needing encouragement to be more assertive.

• Being lazy, and inclined to let others do the work, if you can get away with it. The one who actually *wants* to be a passenger.

• Finding it difficult to give, or receive, instructions or disciplinary warnings to/from other students - seeing it as 'playing teacher'.

• Wanting to do everything democratically because it seems fairer and more comfortable, and then finding that sometimes you just need someone to make a decision. Becoming disorganised, because no-one's really in charge. You're either all indians, or there are too many chiefs.

For any of the above reasons, losing your sense of ownership in the project, and falling into a downward spiral of ever-increasing reluctance and unreliability. Becoming a passenger in the group - a problem for the others.

As I'm sure you can see, these are difficult issues. It's no wonder it's tempting to try to side-track them altogether, by doing everything on your own, if you can. Being able to work well as a member of a team is, however, the key skill employers look for. It's far more important to them than your experience with software, hardware, or creative development of an idea. These things they can teach you through their own training schemes. If, though, you're unable to slot into a production team without causing friction, then you are, I'm afraid, poison, and you won't last long in their employ. So now's your golden opportunity to get good at it - before it starts to really matter.

Some strategies for group work

You need to find ways to balance out the workload between you, so that all of you have plenty of opportunities to generate individual assessment evidence to potential Distinction level, while at the same time avoiding needless duplication of tasks. It doesn't make sense, for example, for everyone to have to write up their own minutes of meetings, or individually storyboard every scene. Neither does it make sense to give only one person in the group the chance to direct, and condemn another to the same, least taxing, role in every location shoot.

This is important not only to ensure harmonious group work, but also for assessment purposes. Remember: the assignment is group-based; but the *assessment* is individual. It's highly unlikely that you will all end up with the same grade. Your tutors will at all times be very concerned to ensure that the way you go about things will generate sufficient portfolio evidence to enable them to reach a grading decision for each of you separately. For this reason, they may sometimes insist upon working methods which seem to you a little odd. Rest assured, they have your best interests at heart. Where they don't prescribe a modus operandi, here are some suggestions:

> • Rotate the role of minute-taker at planning meetings, so that you all take it in turns to make notes and distribute copies. You could rotate the role of Chair as well, so everyone has responsibility at least once for controlling the meeting and getting through the agenda.

> • If you are required to pitch your proposal, work together on the proposal, then split up the presentation between you, so each of you takes a section.

> • Ensure you all contribute to the storyboard development process. You could do this by having every member of the group create a rough draft storyboard for each scene as you work on it, and bring it to a meeting. You all then look at the storyboards together and either

settle on a winner or devise a revised storyboard that combines ideas from the drafts. This becomes the version you take forward to production - *but you don't throw away the drafts.* They are valuable individual evidence for your portfolio: and that's where they should go. For assessment purposes, it makes no difference whether your version was the 'chosen' one or not. What matters is that you have solid evidence of participation in the process.

• Alternatively, you could decide to split up the storyboarding work, for instance taking a scene each, following group discussion of the approach to be taken.

• At the shooting stage, give everyone a chance at all of the roles - director, camera operator, sound, lighting, production assistant, and so on. You could split everything up by scene, or by location. Make sure your planning documentation is clear as to who does what, when. Any changes of plan on the day must also be clearly recorded. Your job on the day is strictly to fulfil your role: "I know best" interference with someone else's role must not be allowed. Everyone works to the director's instructions; if your job is sound, you don't start calling the shots on lighting; and so on. The location is not the place for democratic discussion: the location is where you do your job.*

it's highly likely that one of your tutors or assessors will be present for at least some of your location shoots, in order to carry out observation assessments. They will be checking, for instance, your understanding of your role, your professionalism, your attention to health and safety, and so on. You might find it a bit inhibiting, but it's actually very useful, especially in the early stages, in helping the team maintain a good working discipline on location. It's a good idea to be observed several times, as you carry out different roles, and have to get used to working together in different ways. If your tutors aren't finding the time to observe you very often, take the initiative, and invite them.

Inevitably this will mean you will be happier with some sections of footage than others. You won't all be equally good at every role. Try not to let your desire to make the product as good as possible affect you too much, though. At the end of the day, the purpose is for each of you to achieve the best grade they can. If the product ends up a little uneven in some respects, that is honest evidence enabling fair assessment.

Similarly at the editing stage, split the sections up so that everyone has a go at rough-cuts, fine-cuts, grading and sound design. Again, make sure to write down who does what for each section.

4: Pre-production

Planning

If you are new to video production, you probably expect to spend most of your available time out on location, acquiring your footage. Asked to put a figure on it, people who haven't done it before usually suggest something like 10% pre-production planning, 70% shooting, and 20% editing as a reasonable allocation of time.

Completely wrong. Planning, pre-production tasks and general organisational issues will eat up huge amounts of your time; and editing also will usually take you a lot longer than you expect. The result is that the acquisition window gets squeezed in the middle to the smallest window you can manage. Acquisition is also the most costly stage of the project, so budget considerations will force you to keep your shooting days to a minimum. Something like 60% planning, 15% acquisition, 25% editing is much more realistic.

The production file

Every aspect of your pre-production work should be documented and kept together so that all information is readily to hand. Your production file is where you keep your scripts, storyboards, notes of meetings, schedule sheets, location recce sheets, location permissions agreements, cast and crew contact information, and budget calculations.

Although you could just collect everything together on your iPad, it's often easier to have a hard copy available in a ring-binder. When you're trying to sort something out, and you're having to riffle back and forth between budgets, storyboards, and minutes of meetings, the iPad interface can be more of an irritation than a help.

A complex production may require additional documentation, such as shot breakdown sheets, contracts, release forms, etc, and it's handy to have a source of ready-made form templates on your iPad. Such a source is *Cinema Forms*, which comes with a starter collection of basic forms, and many more purchasable from its shop. It allows you to customise the forms with your own company logos, and you can also (with the paid-for Pro version) print them or share them as pdf's with each other via Dropbox or email.

Meetings

Obviously, if you're doing a project as a group, you'll need to engage in a great deal of discussion at all stages. To keep everything tight and well organised, and also to ensure that you're generating the all-important assessment evidence you need for your portfolio, you should ensure that all your important discussions are carried out in a formal way and properly recorded. Keep the hurriedly-convened chats in the canteen to a minimum.

Proper meetings should include everyone, and have an agenda. Someone should take notes, and circulate them afterwards, so everyone has a record of what was decided. That doesn't mean you have to write down word for word what everyone says. The important things are the outcomes of the discussions, such as, for instance:

- the progress review: issues that arose;

- for each item of the agenda, what we decided;

- the result of a vote;

- tasks allocated at this meeting - who is to do what, by when.

Action minutes, as they're called, are fine. They should be dated, and should note who was there and who was absent. Each of you should have a copy. File them in your portfolios as part of your planning evidence.

You'll find in your discussions that some of the time you will be deciding how to go about things - *forward planning*; some of the time you will be more concerned with keeping on top of things - *monitoring*; and some of the time you will be assessing how things went - *review*. The balance between these three will shift as your project develops, but most of your meetings should give some time to each.

Important meetings where issues need to be thrashed out, or ideas bounced around, are best held face-to-face, in an appropriate private room. Interim meetings - progress monitoring on agreed tasks, for instance - could be held online, for instance via video conferencing, chat-room or blog. So long as there's the portfolio evidence that the meeting took place, there's nothing wrong with using the technology to save having to make an inconvenient journey.

Research

Research means finding things out for yourself, in an organised and professional way. It's a necessary component of pre-production; and, once you get into it, can become one of the most absorbing and enjoyable. There are different kinds of research you will need to undertake, and different ways of going about it. All of them, though, require you to be systematic, persistent and thorough.

Research vs plagiarism

Imagine for a moment that you are shooting a Jane Austen adaptation, and this is an extract from your costume research file:

> 'Pride and Prejudice' was first published in 1813, and the story is set around 1800. | The class system of the early 1800's was very important in defining who a person was. The upper-class were seen as the elite, a small and exclusive percentage of the population that were most easily distinguished by their superior attitudes, keen sense of fashion and elaborate clothes. These men and women were not subject to the hard labor that many others in the working and lower classes were, and their clothes reflected their privileged lifestyles. The women were distinguished by their strict clothes that consisted of laces, corsets, veils, and gloves so that their bodies were properly covered. The men, referred to as "gentlemen," wore strict fitting shirts with ruffled collars, petty coats, and tall boots. Jane Austen's lifetime was during these era, so Pride and Prejudice was deeply influenced by this fashion sense. | For our Mr Darcy, therefore, I would suggest something like……(etc).

This is plagiarism. A chunk of text has been copied from a website and pasted in without any indication of which words are your own, and which are quotation (I have inserted vertical lines (|) to mark the beginning and end of the cut-and-paste). It is doubly wrong to do things this way, because (a) it looks as though you are trying to pass it off as all your own work - so it will, if spotted, be regarded as cheating; and (b) it reads as though you haven't actually *done* any research: you are simply writing what you think is correct, without bothering to check your facts. You will be heavily penalised for this - and perhaps disqualified altogether.

The way to do it is to insert direct quotations from other sources (books, websites etc) into your text in a way that clearly separates the two. Use indentation, and perhaps even a different font. Then make sure you fully identify the source, so that your assessors can go to it and check it for themselves. The full

URL for a website; author, title and publisher for a book. Like this:

'Pride and Prejudice' was first published in 1813, and the story is set around 1800. According to student research carried out at the University of Washington:

> The class system of the early 1800's was very important in defining who a person was. The upper-class were seen as the elite, a small and exclusive percentage of the population that were most easily distinguished by their superior attitudes, keen sense of fashion and elaborate clothes. These men and women were not subject to the hard labor that many others in the working and lower classes were, and their clothes reflected their privileged lifestyles. The women were distinguished by their strict clothes that consisted of laces, corsets, veils, and gloves so that their bodies were properly covered. The men, referred to as "gentlemen," wore strict fitting shirts with ruffled collars, petty coats, and tall boots. Jane Austen's lifetime was during these era, so Pride and Prejudice was deeply influenced by this fashion sense.
> (http://staff.washington.edu/cgiacomi/courses/english200/finalprojects/websitev/Introduction.html)

For our Mr Darcy, therefore, I would suggest something like......(etc)

Types of research

There are three kinds of research that you will need to undertake, in preparation for production: *content research*, *production research*, and *market research*.

Content research

Content research typically includes things like:

- Script development research for a drama (e.g. the symptoms of arsenic poisoning);

- Background/historical research for a documentary (e.g. when the pit closed, and why);

- Sourcing photographs, documents etc. for a documentary (- and clearing copyright for their use);

- Costume and props (historical accuracy) research for a period drama or music video;

- Background and briefing research for interviews;

- Sourcing contributors (e.g. to a 'My Town' type programme);

- Finding appropriate background music (and clearing copyright).

The above example of costume research for 'Pride and Prejudice', while *relevant* research, isn't *good* research. Although the University of Washington sounds like an impressive source, the quotation is actually from a piece of junior student coursework. It's interesting - but it isn't, by itself, authoritative. You should always go to more than one source, in order to check the accuracy of the information, and include at least one authoritative source (in this case, an encyclopaedia of fashion, or a scholarly work on costume in the Regency period).

Production research

Production research typically includes things like:

- Finding locations. Checking out whether you need to get permission to film. Estimating travelling times to/from locations. Estimating setting-up and striking times;

- Finding sources of costumes, props etc.;

- Finding your talent (actors, presenters etc.);

- Checking availability of contributors/interviewees;

- Checking/making transport arrangements;

- Checking factors that might affect filming (e.g. market day, early closing day, roadworks).

Your content research (above) on early nineteenth-century dress fashion would lead naturally on to your having to do some production research: checking out what is available in local costume hire and fancy dress shops, and getting some prices. You would then take your findings back to a planning meeting for discussion.

Market research

Whatever kind of video you're intending to make, you're not making it just for yourself. In your proposal, you will need to demonstrate that you have a good understanding of the audience it's aimed at, and a clear distribution strategy for reaching that audience. You must also show you have thought realistically about how much it will cost to make, where this money might come from, and how you plan to recoup your costs and possibly make a profit. Your means of initial funding and of eventual distribution may be the same (as with a Film4 commission), or different (as with an independent production funded by private investors, and uploaded to YouTube, or burned direct to DVD). Either way, all this requires you to undertake another layer of research, this time enabling you to pitch your idea as a solid business proposition in the video marketplace.

Your market research, therefore, must address three aspects:

> • Target audience - demographic segment, psychographic profile, test screenings etc. *(see Task, below)*;

> • Funding - commissioning bodies, private sources 'angels', grants, etc.;

> • Distribution - broadcast, festivals, DVD sales, YouTube, Vimeo, etc..

Task: research about research

In the section above on market research, I threw in some terminology in parentheses about target audience that you might not be familiar with. Your task is to Google around them to make sense of them. See what you can find, then compare notes. Feel free to follow links and type in variations on search criteria. Start with the following:

> • Audience research;

> • Qualitative and quantitative research methods;

> • Demographic segmentation;

> • Psychographic profiling;

> • Designing questionnaires.

When you've done, you should be a lot more clued-up about how to do audience research; and you will have also had some practice at using the secondary research method.

Research methods

Your individual evidence of participation in the research process must show that you have used both *primary* and *secondary* methods of gathering and sifting information.

Primary research

This means new research that you yourself have devised; for example:

- Going to costume hire shops to view what is available and check prices;

- Location surveys (e.g. possibilities of using different locations for externals and internals);

- Contacting contributors, interviewees etc. to check their availability and suitability;

- Sourcing photographs, documents etc for use in your video;

- Audience research questionnaires;

- Audience research focus group discussions;

- Test screenings;

- Market research questionnaires.

Secondary research

(sometimes called 'desk research') is what you are doing when you find things out from existing publications, such as books, newspapers, and the internet. For example:

- Script development research;

- Historical and background research;

- Facts, figures, statistical data, such as advertising revenues from YouTube streams.

Divide it up between you

It would obviously be silly to duplicate each other's efforts. It is right to divide the workload up and assign responsibility to each other for the various research tasks that will arise. However, you should bear in mind that each of you needs to have individual evidence of having undertaken *both primary and secondary research*, and to have contributed to the research development of *the content*, the *production logistics*, and the *funding and marketing strategy*. Be careful how you divide up the research between you, therefore. Don't leave anyone with holes in their assessment evidence. It's a good idea to keep track of it with a checklist of some kind (see below).

Make sure each of you has something in every box. That way, the work is divided up fairly, in a way that protects everybody's interests when it comes to being assessed.

	Hayley	Ben	Waseem	Gita
Primary content research				
Secondary content research				
Primary production research				
Secondary production research				
Primary market research				
Secondary market research				

Research checklist

Proposals & Pitches

A pitch is a sales presentation. What you are selling is your brilliant idea - your proposal. What you want is for someone to offer you a contract and lots of money to turn your idea into a finished media product. This means you have to make a persuasive case as to why they should invest in your idea.

A well-structured proposal should achieve the following objectives:

- Explain the creative content of your idea, so that everyone fully understands what it is you want to make, and in such a way that they get as enthusiastic about it as you are.

- Show that your idea is a good business proposition - that you have a clear, researched understanding of your target audience, and solid reasons why you are offering your idea to them, rather than to someone else.

- Include a budget breakdown, to justify why you are asking for the amount of money you propose.

- Suggest possible distribution strategies, with example profit forecasts.

Pitching your proposal effectively means you have to do more than just hold a round-table discussion. People will get a much better idea of what your film will be like if you can show, as well as tell. Figures and statistics are also much better presented visually, rather than as rows of numbers. An all-singing, all-dancing performance making good use of presentation software is what's called for.

On the iPad, *Keynote*, Apple's iWork equivalent to *Powerpoint*, is the most obvious contender (Powerpoint, which is part of Microsoft Office, is not currently available as an iPad app). Alternatively, you could, of course, put together your presentation with Powerpoint on a desktop PC. Either software will allow you to put together a set of text slides, and include video clips, audio clips, tables, photographs, and so on, and run it as a live slide-show with a choice of transitions from one slide to the next.

You might, however, want to consider *Presentation Link* as a more flexible alternative. You can use it to set up a linear slide-show, just as with Powerpoint and Keynote; but you can also insert link buttons to take you quickly back and forth between sections of your presentation. This means you're not tied to a linear format. If someone interrupts with a question related to an earlier or later slide, you can jump straight to it and deal with the question without having to scroll through all the other slides. This is especially helpful at the end of your presentation, when you call for questions.

Giving a presentation: the golden rules:

• Don't talk to your slides, talk to your audience. Maintain eye-contact. Be friendly - smile.

• Don't fill your slides with blocks of text. Your audience will concentrate on reading, rather than on listening to what you are saying. Stick to bullet-points. The rest should be in your head, not on the screen.

• Bullet points do two things: they help the audience grasp the structure of your presentation, and stay with you; and they remind you what the next thing is you have to say.

• Be prepared to pause after a change of slide, especially with complex information, to allow people to take in the slide content, before carrying on.

• Don't read from the screen (other than to clarify which bullet-point you are on). A set of slides is not a script.

• Allow people to interrupt with a question, if they wish. If it's not a complex issue, deal with it immediately. If it's something you will be coming onto later, say so; then when you get to the relevant section, refer back to the earlier question, to show you haven't forgotten it.

• Always leave time for questions at the end. Invite questions positively: don't appear reluctant to engage. Give them time - there's usually a bit of a pause to start with.

Scriptwriting

All scripts should be written using industry-standard screenplay formatting conventions. This is especially important if you are on a vocational course, as the whole point of such courses is to learn how to do things professionally, so that you have relevant skills for employment. This means you should really be using appropriate software: even though in theory you could set up your own template, typing scripts in Pages won't get you anywhere in the industry.

The best-known are *Final Draft* and *Celtx*, and both are available as apps for the iPad. There are others available - but be wary of cheap and free apps from small developers; they may be liable to crash or not work properly.

Have a look at some professional examples:

http://www.scriptsandscribes.com/sample-screenplays/

As you can see, they are typed in 12 point Courier, lines are double-spaced, and everything runs down the centre of the page, so that there are wide margins on both sides. There are strict rules for layout and font styles; and keyboard shortcuts for character, dialogue, etc. automatically select for each the correct indenting, capitalisation, and so on, so that all you need to do is type in the words.

Storyboarding

A storyboard looks rather like a comic strip, though there are significant differences. They seem superficially similar because the comic strip and graphic novel generally follow the narrative conventions of film and video, such as significant close-up, reaction shot, point-of-view shot, and so on. This is what makes these publications more like printed TV programmes than novels. However, remember you are not drawing a comic when working on a video storyboard. You don't have to produce detailed, coloured-in artwork. (It is, in fact, a tell-tale sign of a student who doesn't understand how to do it, that they spend hours producing beautiful, artistic frames - but when you examine them closely, they aren't really going to work as sequences). The task isn't about artwork - you don't have to be good at drawing. You are not being assessed on the artistic quality of the work. Stick-people will do. Remember, a storyboard is a tool: its purpose is functional, not decorative. It fulfils two practical functions: in pre-production planning (for visualisation), and in acquisition.

For visualisation

A picture is worth a thousand words. When you plan, for example, a scene of a TV drama, you have to think how to convey the scene as a sequence of shots.

You can't just lock the camera on a wide shot on a tripod and ask the actors to act in front of it. That would record the action, certainly - but that's not how it's done. The camera is active, not passive, in constructing the narrative. You have, for each scene, to decide how many shots you want to use, and what these shots will be - building shots into sequences that construct the action with appropriate emphasis, pace, dramatic impact. Consider, for example, a typical moment from a Hitchcock-style crime thriller:

> *We see a hand slowly turning a door handle and pushing the door open inwards. Fran is standing in the hotel bedroom with her back to the door. The unknown assailant glides swiftly towards her, grasps her around the waist, and presses a cotton pad over her mouth and nose. Fran attempts to struggle, and half-screams. then loses consciousness.*

There are many possible ways of filming this simple sequence. The art lies in making the choices effectively. Try thinking it through by yourself as a series of shots, then, in your group, share and discuss each others' ideas.

Having thought it through in your mind's eye, how then do you best make a note of your thoughts for yourself, or communicate your intention to others? You could explain everything in words - but you will very quickly realise that words aren't precise enough. What, for instance, do you mean by 'a medium close-up'? It could mean any one of a vast range of subtly-different possibilities between mid-shot and close-up. A picture, however, shows precisely how you want the shot framed: we see the size, the angle, the mise-en-scene, the mise-en-shot, instantly, with a precision that might, indeed, take hundreds of words to explain. And this is just for one shot! Imagine how long a set of instructions for a whole sequence would be!

So you draw pictures. It makes sense, for a visual medium, yes? Each single frame of your drawing stands for a shot, of whatever duration. Camera movements within-shot, such as zooms and pans, can be indicated on the drawing with text or arrows; but every change of shot is a new frame. Frame by frame, you are thinking through how to shoot the film. When finished, it then becomes your 'director's bible' for acquisition. As Hitchcock once famously remarked, the creative work on a film is finished once the storyboard is completed. The shooting stage is a purely mechanical process of realising the storyboard on film with real actors.

In acquisition

The second function of a storyboard is as a production tool. It is your camera operator's instruction sheet on how to acquire each shot. It is important that s/he approaches this in a disciplined way, and obeys the storyboard. It is most definitely not part of the camera-operator's role to make 'creative decisions' as s/he goes along. Unless something is clearly very wrong with the proposed shot and requires discussion, then the storyboard should be followed to the letter without question. This isn't just because the director's vision rules: there is a very practical issue to consider. Films shot on several locations are normally shot out of sequence, so that all the required shots for each location are filmed at the same time, regardless of their place in the finished film. This means you only have to set up and strike for each location once, thus saving time and money. It may not be immediately apparent to the camera-operator how all the bits of the jigsaw are to fit together, when several sequences from different sections of the film are shot on the same day; but, if each sequence is shot correctly as required on the storyboard, then all will be well at the edit.

iPad tools for storyboarding

Time was when you had to hand-draw storyboard frames on a pad of templates. If you weren't an artist (or you didn't have the time to work slowly), that meant cartoon-ish frames of stick people. You can still do it that way if you prefer, but the iPad provides you with a range of neater methods.

If you have a talent for graphic art, and you want to draw all your frames by hand, then there are plenty of note-taking and drawing apps to choose from in the app store. I like *Penultimate*, a simple and elegant app which feels very natural to use, because there's no latency between the stroke action and the appearance of the image on the screen. It doesn't come with a storyboard template, but there are plenty available for it on the internet, or you can import your own as a custom paper. Don't forget, if you're taking this route, you'll also need a stylus.

If you prefer taking photographs to drawing sketches, there's a rather expensive but well-designed app called *Storyboard Composer HD*, which converts still photographs to thumbnail storyboard frames, and allows you to add camera movement instructions, text, and even audio. When you've finished, you can play it back as a slide-show. You can take the photographs within the app, or you can import images from your photo library. This is a very good method for those new to film-making, because the process teaches you to think in shots and sequences. It's obvious, when you play a sequence back, whether it works or not. If you get it wrong, you can always re-arrange the thumbnails.

Finally, if you can't draw, but you still prefer to storyboard at your desk, rather than have to organise your group to go to locations and pose for photographs (time-consuming in itself), then you might want to consider working with models or pre-drawn illustrations. While you can get sophisticated apps such as

Moviestorm that allow you to manipulate characters in a 3D virtual environment, my own preference is for a straightforward 2D sketch-creating app such as *Storyboards Premium*, which is much faster to work with, and does everything you need for what is, after all, a pre-production, not production, task.

Storyboards Premium

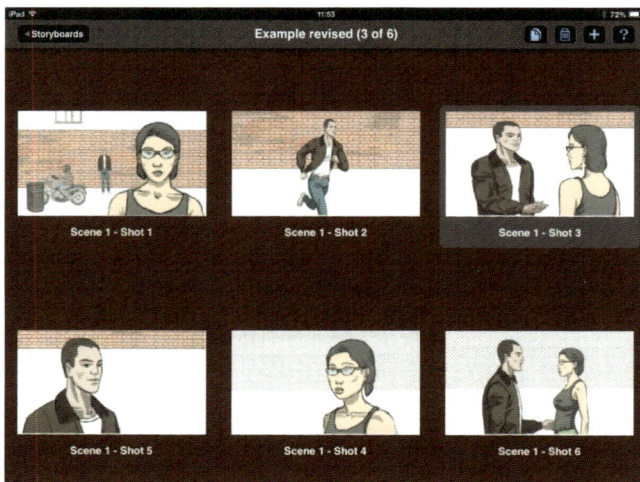

Building a sequence in Storyboards Premium

Storyboarding conventions

Shot size

Extreme close up (ECU)

Two shot (2S)

Big close up (BCU)

Medium long shot (MLS)

Close up (CU)

Long shot (LS)

Medium close up (MCU)

Very long shot (VLS)

Mid shot (MS)

35

Shot angle

High angle (H/A)

Over the shoulder (OTS)

Low angle (L/A)

Conveying movement in-shot

Pan right

Track right

Pan left

Track left

Dolly in

Dolly out

Tilt up

Tilt down

Instructions

Instructions often confirm the shot size and angle. Keep other text brief, but include anything that isn't self-explanatory in the illustration, such as a significant sound effect, or a precise point in the dialogue for a camera movement.

Shots and sequences

Don't think in shots: try to think in sequences. A sequence is a set of shots which together create a single 'moment' in your unfolding story. Scenes are made up of sequences, and sequences are made up of shots. The 'Hitchcock' example above is a sequence, and would probably consist of about four to six shots. The standard building-blocks of sequences are:

> • *the establishing shot* - a long shot or very long shot which is usually the first shot in a sequence at the start of a new scene. It shows us the 'big picture': where we are, who is in the scene, and how they are placed in relation to each other. Without an initial establishing shot, a series of close-ups might not make much sense to us.

> • *the cutaway* - a shot inserted into a sequence that give us privileged information on what is about to happen. The shot of the hidden

attacker in the bushes, or the innocent cyclist just around the corner from the speeding car.

• *the reaction shot* - a shot showing us the emotional effect of preceding dialogue or action. The eyes widening in fear, the suspicious frown, the rictus of frozen panic as the car teeters on the edge of the cliff...

• *shot reverse shot* - a technique for filming two people looking at or talking to each other. The shots making up the sequence are filmed with the characters facing in opposite directions. The shots are the same size (often a medium close up), with matched eyelines. It will usually be preceded by an establishing two-shot; but even without this we assume the two people are looking at each other. The classic example is the conversation in a restaurant.

• *the point-of-view shot* - in which the camera momentarily becomes one of the characters. These are usually inserted in a sequence between an objective establishing shot and a reaction shot, and often signalled by being hand-held.

• *the match on action* - a sequence of shots cut together to create a sense of continuity. For example, a car enters the frame right, and exits left. In the next shot, the car enters the frame at a different location right, and turns into a driveway centre.

• *the inter-cut* - a shot or sequence from one location inserted into another. For example, flashback moments in psychological dramas.

• *the cross-cut* - shots from two different sequences involving different characters at different locations, cut repeatedly together to suggest that they are happening at the same time (this is known as *parallel action*). For example, the bank robbers blowing the safe open, cross-cut with the police car rushing to the scene. Telephone conversation sequences which cut from one receiver to the other are another example of a cross-cut.

Visualisation, style and meaning

A cut is virtually invisible to us most of the time. We almost never notice cuts, unless we are consciously looking for them. A sequence might consist of many shots, from many different distances and angles, but if each and every individual shot is static (i.e. the scene is alive, but the camera does not move), and the shots are simply butted together, the sequence is generally perceived as a seamless continuity. We are, however, consciously aware of in-shot camera movements such as zooms, pans, steadicam tracking and shaky hand-held shots. Un-natural actions like zoom (which we cannot achieve in real-life with our eyes alone) are particularly noticeable, and serve to remind us that we are watching a film. They act as barriers to our absorption in the narrative. For this reason, the usual preferred approach in film and television drama is to use tripod or dolly-mounted cameras, and to build sequences out of static shots, cut together. Cut - cut - cut - cut. Zooms and pans are only used if there is a very good reason for it, and then only rarely. For the same reason, 'art' films wishing to adopt the Brechtian approach of self-conscious, self-referential revelation of the artifice involved in narrative construction, tend to make much more deliberate use of techniques that draw attention to the film-making process, and disrupt the viewer's emotional engagement with the story and characters - including frequent use of extreme devices such as the whip-pan and the jump-cut.

Some techniques have, over time, become 'visual metaphors', which we have automatically come to understand in a particular way, depending on our experience of previous films. For example, slow-motion used to mean only one thing: the sentimental 'aah' moment as lovers or families are reunited, or characters recall idyllic scenes from their childhood. However, since Sam Peckinpah's *The Wild Bunch*, and subsequent ultraviolent movies such as Quentin Tarantino's *Reservoir Dogs* and *Pulp Fiction*, it has also come to signify an invitation to the audience to share in the director's sadistic relish of moments of extreme visceral brutality.

Other such visual metaphors include:

> •*shooting a scene in black-and-white* within a film which is otherwise shot in colour. We generally understand this to signify a flashback, or more generally in some way 'from the past'.

> • *hand-held camerawork*. This usually signifies a point-of-view shot: this isn't just a shot, this is a person (frequently a person I can't see. I don't know who this is, but he's stalking her…). If it isn't a point-of-view shot then it just looks amateurish.

So: hand-held camerawork, together with unmotivated hosing around, zooming in/out rather than cutting (it's shot 1 forever…), and poor pixel-quality and sound, signifies 'this is amateur camcorder or mobile-phone footage I am now watching'. This is what made *The Blair Witch Project* such a sensational success on its first release: the whole film appeared to consist of amateur footage shot by the characters themselves, and had therefore to be a true record of actual events. We, the audience, were mis-cued by the visual metaphors being employed; it was a cinematic conjuring-trick (and, like all novelty tricks, it only works once. We are now wise to the deception).

Mise-en-scene, mise-en-shot

Mise-en-scene

...The film opens with an establishing shot of Melanie in her kitchen, She is frying fish-fingers. The kitchen is small, the units are flat-pack melamine, the cooker is elderly, and the limited workspace is mostly taken up with a clutter of dirty pans and dishes.

...The film opens with an establishing shot of Melanie in her kitchen. She is spooning drop-scone batter onto a griddle. The kitchen is large and tidy, with hand-painted designer units.

...The film opens with an establishing shot of Melanie in her kitchen. She is taking a loaf of bread out of her Aga. The furniture consists mostly of free-standing antique pine - a Welsh dresser, a table, a butler sink, and an overhead hanging rail of pots, utensils and dried herbs.

That's mise-en-scene. In the first two seconds of the film, before anything is said, we already know a great deal about Melanie. Mise-en-scene is really, really important. Never compose a shot without paying attention to the background around the characters. Always dress the set.

This means, when you are making your video project on a student budget (i.e. no budget), and you are having to film in each other's homes, because there's nowhere else you can use, you shouldn't just accept the first offer from a kind parent and then cease to think about it. If you have the luxury of more than one kitchen you are allowed to use, then your choice should be based on which one most nearly fits your characterisation of Melanie, *not* which one is closest to college. If you make a wrong choice, you risk sending mixed messages about location and character, and weakening your story.

Also, remember you don't have to use the same location for everything. If the action moves from the kitchen to the lounge, we assume it is the same house; but that doesn't mean you have to *film it* in the same house. Similarly, exterior shots can be taken in different locations from interior shots. If your script calls for an isolated house in the country, but your only available kitchen is on an inner-city estate, then film the interior shots and exterior shots separately. Take Melanie through the front door of one house into the kitchen of another. Create Melanie's fictional house from six different real houses, if you like - why not?

Having dressed the set, what about Melanie? In each of the above three scenarios, what kinds of clothes would you expect her to be wearing? Unless there's a good storyline reason why not, that's how she should be dressed. This, too, is mise-en-scene.

Then there's how you light the scene. In cinema, establishing the mise-en-scene includes paying attention to the way the intensity, direction and quality of the lighting affects the mood and meaning of a scene. Comedies, for example, tend to be shot in bright lighting; romantic or emotional stories favour softer lighting; while a sense of unease or menace is usually created by the use of hard directional lighting with deep shadows, most famously in Film Noir.

If you are shooting a no-budget video in a friend's house with limited equipment, you probably won't have as much control as you would like over the available light. Your friend's parents' generosity might be stretched if you started moving the furniture around, or setting up redheads. However, that doesn't mean you just have to accept the lighting conditions as you find them.

For instance, Melanie 1 (above)'s grubby melamine kitchen will look more unpleasant and down-at-heel in the evening, lit by the overhead fluorescent strip-light, than it does in the daytime. On the other hand, Melanie 3's farmhouse kitchen will look most rustically nostalgic in morning sunlight.

How about your scene in the lounge? You can use natural daylight, or you can draw the curtains and use artificial light. If the latter, do you choose the overhead ceiling light or the table lamps? That's three very different moods, for the same room.

Mise-en-shot

This refers to the contribution to mise-en-scene made by choices of camera position, camera movement, length of shot and pace of editing. Consider, for example, the extended use of point-of-view camera technique in establishing the chilling mood of David Carpenter's *Hallowe'en*.

An eye-level objective wide shot of Melanie in her kitchen, filmed from inside the kitchen, simply establishes Melanie as a character. A shot of Melanie in her brightly-lit kitchen, taken at an angle from just outside her uncurtained window at night, establishes both Melanie *and* the unseen presence of an intruder or stalker.

How to construct a sequence

How do you decide how to shoot a sequence? How many shots do you need? What kind of shots? What's the thinking process that enables you to make these decisions?

Take a simple example - a moment on film. *A man fills a glass of water from a tap and drinks*. Maybe not a hugely significant moment, but still requiring decisions from the director.

You could, of course, simply lock your iPad off on a medium long shot and allow it to passively record the action taking place in front of its lens - but that's the one thing you wouldn't do, right? Why not? It's boring. *Why* is it boring? Because it's not involved, and so not involving. You would only ever use such a technique if you were deliberately wishing to indicate to the viewer that the seeing eye is a security camera. The locked-off camera is merely a recording device; whereas the camera in cinema and television is a *storyteller*. The locked-off shot is boring because it is showing the act of drinking with a distanced objectivity which fails to stimulate our interest. What we need to do is get to the emotional centre of the moment, the heart of the moment that connects with our human sympathies in some way - because people are interested in people.

So now, going back to our little sequence. What is it about? What is it *really* about? A man drinking a glass of water? No. It's about *being thirsty*. It's about *having thirst satisfied*. Through showing externals, we reveal internals.

Once we have realised this, we know how it must be filmed. The shots select themselves:

> *An establishing wide shot to start with, showing us the man, the glass, the tap, the mise en scene. Then quickly moving to a close-up, maybe low-angle, and if possible against the light, to capture the beads of sweat on his face as he gazes longingly down. Next we follow his gaze, as shot three shows us what he is looking so longingly at, with a matching reverse shot of the tap filling the glass. Cut to a different angle with the glass in the foreground as the glass is lifted. Squeeze and tighten with a BCU of the lips, the edge of the glass, and the undulating throat, and finally back to a more neutral MCU to capture the experience of relief.*

As I said, not necessarily a major crisis-point in the film; more likely an entirely unimportant moment - but nonetheless a building-brick which has to grab our attention, hold us, tell us something about character, make sense as a human moment in this story of human lives. We have felt the moment - what it is to be thirsty. We *empathise*.

When we understand the emotional centre of the moment, we know how to film it. You have to ask The Actor's Question: "What's my motivation?" Without knowing this, the actor doesn't know how to play the moment. The director says to the actor, "OK. Scene 56. You pour yourself a glass of water and drink. That's it." The actor says, "What's my motivation? There are a zillion ways of drinking a glass of water. Which one do you want?" The director says, "You're thirsty." *Now* the actor knows how to play the scene. It might be a very significant moment, or a trivial detail - but it has to make sense. In exactly the same way, the camera needs to be told *why* this moment is part of the story. That's the difference: the security camera is a recording device: the movie camera is *motivated*.

If you fully grasp this principle, from this simple moment of drinking a glass of water, then you will be able to visualise and storyboard any sequence.

Narrative and genre

The way you tell the story (*narrative*) depends on what kind of story it is (*genre*). All storytelling has conventions, and the good storyteller understands not just what the story is, but how it should be told. This applies just as much to the flying pixel as to the printed page.

Genre refers to a type (of novel, film, television programme etc), and to the various conventions that make up the characteristics of that type. Genre works on two levels: commonalities, and contrasts. A 'police procedural', for example, is a genre (strictly speaking, a sub-genre of the genre 'crime fiction'). Morse, Frost, and Midsomer Murders are all police procedurals. All of them follow the process of police detection, from the initial committing of the crime or discovery of the victim, up to the point of arrest. The central characters in this type of story are always police officers, and they are usually shown as hampered by 'stuffed-shirt' senior officers, and as having dysfunctional personal relationships, owing to the pressures of the job. These things they have in common, and are what make them instantly pigeonhole-able.

However, our appreciation of them is also heavily influenced by the ways in which, without departing from type, they differ from each other. Consider the marked contrast between two other police procedurals: Wallander, and Inspector Montalbano. Wallander is typical of Scandinavian crime fiction (often dubbed 'Nordic Noir') - grim, dark, obsessive and relentless. Inspector Montalbano, by contrast, never lets the pursuit of a criminal get too much in the way of his enjoyment of a good meal, preferably with an attractive woman. All talk stops when the pasta arrives. It is the product of a sunnier clime, and a more sensual, laid-back culture.

Narrative refers to the structure of a story. There are many ways of telling a story. The most straightforward is to start at the beginning, with one situation and one set of characters, and move chronologically forward to the end. This is called a *linear narrative*, and it is what we are most used to in, for instance, television plays and Hollywood films. It is also the most common way of telling a factual story in a documentary, as it is engaging and easy to follow. A more complex linear narrative may make use of flash-backs or flash-forwards, but it is still essentially linear. It's the default position for storytelling.

However, not all stories follow this pattern. You could, for instance, set up two sets of storylines and character relationships, and follow each separately as the story unfolds. The two stories are, of course, connected, and the nature of the connection is the heart of the story. This is revealed at the end. This type of structure is called *parallel narrative*.

Another common structuring device is the *multi-strand narrative*, in which many separate storylines are set up with different sets of characters. Major characters in one storyline might appear as minor characters in another, but the storylines are not necessarily otherwise connected. The stories are not moving to one single dénouement. This type of narrative structure is best known in television soap operas, such as EastEnders and Coronation Street, but it is also the way many fly-on-the-wall documentaries and reality TV shows are constructed.

Many genres are strongly associated with particular narrative techniques, and there are usually good reasons for this. Soap operas, for example, are essentially about the interwoven dramas of everyday life: the beating heart of a community. To do this, it needs to set up many viewpoints, and follow the many events which make up the daily lives of its characters. There is no beginning, no middle, no end. Storylines come and go, but life moves on. Interestingly, some soaps have occasionally produced 'specials', which concentrate on one particularly compelling storyline; in doing so, however, the narrative becomes linear, and the episode becomes less of a 'slice of life' and more of a theatrical drama. For this reason, such specials are infrequent.

Similarly, the police procedural tends to use a linear narrative, restricted to the police perspective upon events. The reason for this is so that we are not given privileged knowledge, so that we enter into the game of trying to guess who the villain is before the police get there. Seeing the crime take place, or being shown scenes of the villains plotting to evade capture, would 'spoil' the story.

You should, therefore, think of narrative and genre as inter-related. The choice of genre should suggest the appropriate narrative approach. You are, of course, allowed to break the rules - but you should only do so after careful consideration of what the normal conventions are, and why they exist. I have seen many student attempts to produce a 'soap opera' which consist of one single storyline and a linear narrative: it just doesn't work.

Location recces, health & safety, risk assessment

Although it might sometimes be tempting, especially if you don't have much time, you should never just go to a location on the spur of the moment and start shooting. You must always do a location recce first, and complete the appropriate paperwork. This may seem a bit tedious, but there are very good reasons for it:

- You need to plan your shots, so that you deliver an organised and complete set of footage to the edit suite. If you just improvise, the likelihood is that it won't edit together properly. You can't plan shots for a location you haven't yet seen.

- It's an important part of being professional. All employers have a duty of care towards their workforce, and must abide by health and safety regulations. If you were working for a video production company and you were sent out to a location, that location becomes a temporary extension of the workplace. Your employer therefore would need to know what you are doing. In the industry, you wouldn't be allowed to just disappear to an unknown location, without giving your employer the opportunity to check the legalities and insurance; so as a student on a vocational course, you shouldn't, either.

- Your college also has a duty of care, and would be at fault if they allowed you to do anything dangerous, if there was an accident, or if you unwittingly did something illegal. There's a *real* need to know, as well as the role-playing one.

Location recces should be thorough and detailed. Take your time - don't rush it. Make sure you cover the following:

- *Check the general suitability of the location* - does it look right for the scene? Is it OK for sound? - if it's very noisy, it might affect how you mic-up the scene, or you might need to try to find somewhere less noisy.

- *Access to electrical points.* If you are filming indoors, you might prefer to conserve your batteries and plug your iPad into a 13 amp socket. If so, you will need to note where they are, and consider the routing of extension leads.

• *Risk assessment and health & safety check.* You absolutely must do this, and fill in the forms - it's a legal requirement. What are the potential (or actual) hazards; and what are you doing to minimise the risks? For example:

> - the *location itself*: slip hazards, trip hazards, the cliff edge, the pond;
>
> - *your equipment set-up*: trailing cables, lights, the microphone fishpole;
>
> - *risks to talent*: walking across a busy road, stroking a rat, being a rookie reporter 'having a go' at something;
>
> - *risks to crew*: dollying backwards, dollying on uneven ground, high-angle shots, e.g. from the top step of a slide.

•*Legal issues.* Is the location private property? If so, you need to get written permission to film, otherwise you will be trespassing. Be careful about this: many apparently public areas, such as shopping malls and car parks, are actually private property. Is the location part of the public highway? If you are setting up equipment in the street, you may be causing an obstruction. Check first, with the police or community support officers, that they are happy for you to be there.

• *Feasibility in relation to your storyboard*: Can the shots be achieved? (can we get that angle without standing in the pond?) - if not, make notes for revision of your storyboard before shooting.

• *Practicalities*: Where do we park the car? Where are the nearest toilets?

Budgeting & costs

A vital aspect of production planning in the real world is staying in control of your finances and completing your production within budget. That's why college assignments often require you to pitch your proposal, just as a production company would to a commissioning editor. Your pitch will have to include a detailed budget breakdown, which you will have to explain and justify.

Even if you don't have to go through a pitch presentation, assignments will generally set you a fictional cost limit, and require you to use rate cards and 'hire' your equipment, talent, locations, and editing facilities. Nothing will be given to you that would in the real world cost you money - and that includes time. It will be up to you to juggle your finances and decide how many days shooting you can afford, how many hours editing time, and so on.

Having made your initial calculations, it will then be up to you to stay on top of your spending. You can't just draw up your budget and then forget about it. Things never go to plan: sometimes it rains. Every extra day you give to shooting may have to come off something else - editing time, probably - so that you stay within budget. If you get it wrong, you have a problem.

This doesn't mean you fail. Your tutors won't step in and prevent you from completing your editing, just because you've used up your budget. However, they will probably require you to continue monitoring your spending, and provide a final calculation of how much over-budget you are. This will give you a great deal to talk about in your evaluation, especially in the section where you consider how you might do things differently next time (ironically, this could lead to your getting a *higher* grade than you might otherwise have achieved, as a detailed, critical, well-focused evaluation is worth a lot in most assessment schemes).

The best way of setting out a budget is to use a spreadsheet, since it enables you to make changes and re-calculate running sub-totals, thus providing you with a means of monitoring, as well as planning, your spending. Apple's *Numbers* is the obvious choice (*Excel*, part of Microsoft Office, isn't currently available for the iPad). The best way of finding out how to set out your spreadsheet is to have a look at some others. There are plenty of Excel templates available on the internet, many of them free. Just Google something like 'free Excel movie templates', and check out a few. If you find one you like, there's no reason why you shouldn't use it. Numbers will quite happily import Excel documents.

If you're not comfortable with spreadsheets, then you could just set up a tables template in *Pages* and type into that. It just means you will have to update your records of costs and recalculate your running totals manually. There's no requirement for how you format your data, so do whatever works for you.

However you choose to present it on the page (or screen), a budget sheet for a digital video production will typically contain calculations for each stage of the production process separately. For a drama or feature film, for instance, this might include:

Pre-Production	Script and rights Development (storyboarding, location research etc.)		
Production	Equipment hire (by the day, each item listed) Location fees Costumes and props Salaries (per day)		
		Director Talent Crew	
	Production expenses		
		Accommodation Mileage Meals Photocopying Postage	
	Insurance		
		Public liability Equipment	
Post-Production	Facilities hire (per hour) Editor Audio dubbing		
Distribution	Promotion and marketing Advertising		
Contingencies*			

*amounts set aside to cover unexpected extra costs - usually around 10%

A budget for a documentary production would differ in the detail - there would be no requirement for screenplay or costumes, for instance, but there would be more costs incurred in research - but would follow the same general pattern.

Your assignment brief may include fictional rate-cards you have to use for your budgeting. Professional video production isn't normally carried out on an iPad, so commercial rate-cards for equipment hire, for instance, won't be of much use to you. However, there are lots of add-ons for the iPad and iPhone now available, aimed at the independent low-budget film-maker. You can, for instance, get LED video lights, steadicams, tracking rails, dolly carts, stereo microphones, remote controllers that enable you to use an iPad as a teleprompter, clear plastic bags for filming underwater; - think of an item of professional equipment, and there'll probably be an iPad or iPhone equivalent somewhere.

It's not that hard, therefore, to dream up a fictional equipment hire company and make up a rate-card; and that's what you might be required to work with. Obviously, if you don't actually have the equipment, then you'll have to improvise. A monopod or microphone fishpole can double as a tracking rail, for instance. You can use a teleprompter app without the remote controller - it's just a bit more awkward scrolling the text. You can dolly with a skateboard or shopping trolley. For budgeting purposes, though, you should assume you are actually hiring the equipment, rather than making do, and include them in your costs.

Scheduling

Imagine you are shooting a crime thriller. The script requires two interior locations and three exterior locations. You don't want to visit locations more than once or twice if you can help it, as it's inefficient time-wise, and also puts a strain on your budget. You need, therefore, to shoot out of sequence. Your storyboards must be split up and re-ordered, so that you have all the scenes for each location together.

You then need to sort out equipment, props, and talent requirements for each location, so that you have everyone and everything you need for each of the scenes you will be filming.

Two of the locations have limited availability, and you need to work within this.

Your talent are also not all available at any time, because of college class timetabling restrictions, transport difficulties or domestic issues.

You think you've nearly cracked it, when suddenly you discover that one of your locations isn't available anymore on the day you want it, and you have either to move everything for those scenes to a different day, or to a different location.

Back to the drawing board...

Drawing up a shooting schedule isn't something you can just do once, and then it's finished. You're trying to hit a moving target. You think it's all sorted, then one thing changes, and causes a domino effect. It can be a bit of a nightmare, unless you have a properly worked-out system that enables you to move things easily around the board. That's what scheduling software is for, and why you need it.

The industry's favoured (expensive) package for the desktop Mac or PC is *Movie Magic Scheduling*. The company that make it have brought out an app, called *Movie Magic Scheduling To Go* - but beware: it's not a stand-alone app. It's designed as slave software: it has to be linked to the master software to work. If your college has invested in this software for its editing suite, then great - you're working with an industry-standard set-up.

If not, and you want to do all your scheduling on the iPad, then a good alternative app is *ShotList*. Like Movie Magic, you create a set of colour-coded horizontal strips, one strip for each scene. Location, cast etc are entered onto the strip, and you can also import storyboard frames. You can then shuffle the strips like a pack of cards to create your schedule for each day. Out on location, you cross off each storyboard frame as you complete it. When you have completed the scene, you mark it as done, and it greys out. It's the way to do things efficiently, and your fast-track to Distinction for 'planning and monitoring'.

iPad 🔋	15:02	🔋 48%
Projects	**Stripboard**	Schedule

| 6 | **PADDY'S BAR** | p.9 3/8 |
| EXT DAY | Dougal and Bernie park their bikes and enter the bar | Sean, Dave |

| 8 | **PADDY'S BAR** | p.12 3/8 |
| INT DAY | Jimmy wins the card game | Brian, Lucy, Sam, Melanie |

| 7 | **WILLY'S ALLOTMENT** | p.9 2/8 |
| EXT DAY | Willy emerges from his shed, followed by Kathleen | Harry, Sarah |

| 14 | **WILLY'S ALLOTMENT** | p.64 9/8 |
| EXT DAY | The police arrive | Harry, John, Terry |

| END DAY 1 | **Wednesday, Jan 22, 2014** | 2 1/8 |

| 17 | **WILLY'S ALLOTMENT** | p.31 1/8 |
| EXT EVE | Willy wraps up the stash in sacking and stuffs it inside his coat | Harry |

| 11 | **WILLY'S ALLOTMENT** | p.28 9/8 |
| EXT D4N | The hut is broken into and trashed | Sam, Melanie |

| 17 | **BACK GARDEN, PADDY'S BAR** | p.27 7/8 |
| EXT D4N | Mel and Sam run out of the back door, towards and past the camera | Sam, Melanie |

| 17 | **BACK GARDEN, PADDY'S BAR** | p.27 8/8 |
| EXT D4N | Reverse angle, following Sam and Mel as they clamber over the wall | Sam, Melanie, Danny, Josh, Stuart |

| END DAY 2 | **Friday, Jan 24, 2014** | 3 1/8 |

| 3 | **PADDY'S BAR** | p.4 2/8 |
| INT DAY | Barry clears glasses and wipes the bar. Sam enters | Sam, Barry |

| 5 | **PADDY'S BAR** | p.8 1/8 |
| INT DAY | Mel enters, sees Brian and Sam, and signals to Barry | Brian, Sam, Melanie, Barry |

| END DAY 3 | **Monday, Jan 27, 2014** | 0 3/8 |

ShotList

51

5: Production

Single-camera acquisition vs multi-camera acquisition

If you are using just the one iPad for all your acquisition, it means you can't get different shot-angles in real time: you will need to take a stop-start approach, or film scenes more than once. To accomplish a shot-reverse-shot on dialogue (two people having a conversation in the college refectory, for example), you would need to shoot the scene at least twice - once for the 'shot', then again for the 'reverse'. In feature films, the traditional approach is to shoot each scene at least three or four times, first with a 'safety-net' wide-angle, then in medium-shot or shot-reverse-shot, then finally in close-up. The editor then has a choice of framings to select from in order to cut the scene together.

In documentaries, where it is often necessary to film in real time, other strategies have to be employed. Interviews, for example, are usually shot with the camera trained on the interviewee. After the interview, 'noddies', as they are called (reverse-angle shots of the interviewer nodding, smiling, or asking a question), are shot separately, and edited in later. In long interviews it may be possible for the director to discreetly instruct the camera operator to stop filming and move in order to achieve a change of angle upon the interviewee. This would be done at times when the director was sure that nothing vital was being said. If you are shooting 'fly-on-the-wall' with just one camera, then you simply have to accept that you can't capture everything in real time, and take advantages of pauses in the action to move to different camera positions.

If, on the other hand, you have several iPads available, and want to shoot multi-camera, then you can shoot in real time. For drama shoots, it makes the process considerably less time-consuming. Depending on the complexity of your storyboard, you may be able to acquire all the footage you need for a sequence - or even a scene - in a single take. Obviously, you will have to select the camera positions carefully so that they don't appear in each others' shots. Also, it may be necessary to capture sound separately from each camera position, especially if you are shooting extremes of wide-shot and close-up at the same time.

Multi-camera set-ups are particularly helpful for documentaries, as you don't usually have the option to film scenes more than once. If you are shooting, for example, a 100 metre sprint race, they are not going to stop in the middle or do it three times over, just for you. Also, you can't do interviews twice: it doesn't work.

Roles

Director

...has overall responsibility for ensuring the shots are acquired as planned. Makes the decisions, and acts as group leader to the production team. Decides how many takes are needed for each shot. In a drama shoot, is the one who works directly with the actors, explaining how scenes should be played. In a documentary shoot, is the one who liaises with contributors and presenters to clarify what is required of them.

Camera operator

...is the one who operates the camera, obviously; but also has the responsibility for checking that it is in good working order before leaving for the location, for setting it up safely and correctly at the location, reporting any problems with shots to the director, and checking that all camera equipment is returned in good order after the shoot, and nothing is left behind.

Sound recordist

...is the one responsible for getting clean and appropriate sound for every shot. This means making decisions on the choice and placement of microphones or portable recorders, in consultation with the director, and monitoring or checking the recording quality during or after a take. Also responsible for checking that the equipment all works, is set up properly, and is all returned in good order.

Production assistant

...assists the director, principally through (i) logging all shots, so that a record is kept as to how many takes there are for each shot; which takes are/are not thought useable; and why; (ii) taking charge of items such as costumes and props needed for the shoot; and (iii) checking for possible continuity errors during the shoot (such as the sudden dis/appearance of a hat). In a documentary, the PA may also be responsible for getting any necessary last-minute permissions, and for getting release forms signed (for example by participants in street interviews).

Camera operation

Framing conventions

- For a standard talking-head medium close up, the eyes should be about two-thirds of the way up the screen, and there should be some headroom space between the top of the head and the top edge of the screen.

- When framing people in profile, frame them off-centre, so they have 'talking space' in front of them. This is especially important if they are actually talking to another character out of shot.

- Similarly, if the character is moving across the screen, frame them off-centre so they have more screen-space in front of them than behind them.

- If the background of your shot includes a horizon line, don't let it bisect the screen equidistantly: keep it either above or below the centre of the frame.

- Asymmetrical compositions are more interesting than symmetrical ones. Whether filming groups of people or groups of trees or buildings, try to achieve an asymmetrical angle.

- When filming very long shots, an element in the foreground will emphasise depth.

Over-the-shoulder shots and reverse 2-shots

- When filming in medium close up, the person facing the camera should have about two-thirds of the screen space.

- When filming in mid shot, divide the screen-space vertically into thirds, and place the person facing the camera in the centre section, both for main and reverse shots.

Panning and tilting

- Both are swivel actions - so use a tripod.

- Practice a pan before you shoot, to check that the horizon is level at both ends of the pan. If not, you will need to adjust the legs of your tripod.

- To execute a pan, stand facing the end position, then, with your feet firmly planted, swivel your body and the camera to the starting position. This way, you move with the pan from an uncomfortable, to a comfortable, balanced stance.

- To execute a tilt, try similarly to move from an uncomfortable to a comfortable position - from a bent, to a straight back, for example.

- Press record a few seconds before the start of the pan or tilt, and continue to record for a few seconds afterwards. You may need this when you come to edit.

All camera movements in-shot should be motivated. For example, a small boy bumping into the legs of a very tall man would naturally look up to the face gazing irritatedly down at him. A slow tilt-up would be an appropriate and dramatically effective subjective shot at this point. Similarly, in a travel documentary, a pan across a landscape would be appropriate immediately following a medium close up of the presenter gazing out of shot.

Crossing the line (the 180° rule)

'Crossing the line' is the cardinal error to avoid when positioning cameras around action. The line referred to is an imaginary line drawn at 180° along the line of the action. The 180° rule states that all your camera positions must be on the same side of this line. If you break this rule, the footage simply won't edit together properly to match on action.

For example, imagine cowboys chasing Sioux from left to right across the screen. In the first shot, the Sioux ride into frame left (for clarity of explanation, let's call it 'west'), then disappear out of frame right ('east'). The camera is placed at the 'south' point in relation to the action. Then - still shot one - the cowboys ride into frame 'west' and out of frame 'east'. In the second shot, at a different point on the path, and with a different camera position (say, 'south-east'), we again pick up the cowboys 'south-west', and they ride across the screen and out again 'north-east'. Not a problem: we are sticking with them as they chase the Sioux.

Now imagine that we had placed the camera for the second shot on the other, 'north' side of the action, pointing in the opposite direction. The cowboys ride into shot - but this time from the right, and out of shot left. Suddenly they seem no longer to be chasing the Sioux - they seem to be galloping away from them, back the way they came!

Similar problems occur with shot-reverse-shot situations and seated interview set-ups. If you accidentally cross the line, in single-head close-up your characters will seem no longer to be looking at each other, but both looking out of shot in the same direction.

If you do accidentally commit this error, and you only notice it at the editing stage, then the only way out of it is to insert a 'buffer' cutaway or long-shot in between, to smooth the change of camera-direction.

6: Post-production

On the iPad

If you're intending to complete your video entirely on your iPad, then you will need to work within its limitations. You can produce a high-quality, fully professional production just with your iPad - but you will be restricted to fairly basic editing techniques. It's probably not a good idea, therefore, to attempt a type of video production that really requires access to special effects.

For instance, you can't do 'green screen' - i.e. compositing work, digitally inserting one image into another (as with the maps in a TV weather forecast, or the use of model sets in futuristic dramas). If you're planning on shooting, say, a science fiction film, or a music video, or an animation, you may need to consider carefully what will, and what will not, be achievable. You may need to start 'thinking analogue' in the way you go about things.

Having said that, there's a lot you can achieve, and with apps that are much more intuitive to work with than high-end post-production applications for the desktop PC.

Editing

You'll probably be using iMovie, or possibly Pinnacle Studio. Whichever, you'll be able easily to trim clips, butt them end to end in the order you want on a timeline, and apply basic transitions like cut, wipe and dissolve.

You'll have multiple audio tracks, so you can edit and mix your dialogue, music, and sound effects separately. You can use still images as well as video footage, and perform 'Ken Burns' effects (zooming or panning on a still photograph, to make it appear like video footage). In iMovie (but not Pinnacle) you'll be able to have your audio come in before or after the associated video, to create an overlapping scene-change ('J or L cuts'). Pinnacle has a 'montage' facility, allowing you to insert video footage, still images or text into your background footage - as with, for example, mug-shots in title sequences. iMovie, with version 2.0, now offers a similar facility, but is limited to video clips, which can either be inserted as picture-in-picture or placed side-by-side as a split-screen.

Grading

Moving on beyond basic editing, you may want to do some colour-correction to some of your shots to improve continuity, or perhaps to all of your shots in a sequence (or even the entire film) to give it a particular 'look'. For example, you might want all your sequences set in a submarine to have a green-ish tint. This process is called 'grading', and, yes, you can get grading apps for the iPad.

The most generally useful is *VideoGrade*, which is designed as a tool, rather than as a special effect. It has Photoshop-type tools for tint, brightness, contrast and saturation, which enable you to correct problems such as white-balancing inconsistencies between shots. You can also use it to impose an overall tint, level of brightness, and so on, to a scene, or to turn colour footage black-and-white.

VideoGrade

There are also other apps, such as *Cinema FX for Video*, which are special-effects rendering tools - enabling you, for instance, to create vignetting, softening, or glowing effects, suitable perhaps for the creation of alien planets or 'silent film' footage.

Note, though, that grading work on the iPad is restricted to *primary corrections* only (corrections affecting the whole of the image area). If you want to make *secondary corrections* (alterations to specific elements within the frame), you'll have to move over to professional software on a desktop computer.

Sound design

OK - you have all your dialogue audio clips, either recorded together with the video on your iPad, or as separate files from whatever equipment you were using on location to record better-quality sound.

If you're using the embedded sound recorded by the video app, then it will be perfectly in sync with the video material, but there's not much you can do to improve it, unless you export it and then re-import the improved version.

If, on the other hand, you have all your dialogue clips on separate audio files, there's a lot you can do with them. You might want to do some fine editing to remove little glitches or unwanted background sounds (a dog barking, say). You might want to adjust the EQ, or add some echo or a more reverberant acoustic.

Then you may want to add some wildtrack background for atmosphere, and some spot or Foley* effects (that slamming metal door on the submarine, for instance).

Foley: post-production sound effects performed live in a dubbing theatre by a 'Foley artist', rather than sourced from a recording. The sounds of footsteps, for example, must match precisely with the image on the screen, and there's no other practical way of achieving this.

Then you may want to add some music, to help build the tension of the scene.

Finally, you have to balance all these elements together to create a smooth mix.

In Pinnacle Studio, in addition to the sound embedded in the video footage, you have three audio tracks to work with, with volume and fade controls assigned as 'property settings' to each clip you import. iMovie allows one track of background music, one track of other audio content (such as narration), plus up to three simultaneous tracks of sound effects, also with basic volume and fade tools. It's possible, therefore, to work in a limited way just in your video editor to place music and sound effects against dialogue and adjust relative levels. You'll get a much better-crafted result, though, if you work on your clips outside of your video editor, and then import them as finished mixes.

There are two types of audio editor: the digital audio workstation (DAW), and waveform editors; both are available as apps. DAW's are multitrack virtual mixing consoles with signal processing facilities such as reverb, EQ, delay, compression, and so on. This is what you will ideally use to optimise your audio material and create your mix. Waveform editors are for fine-editing of single audio files - for example for removing unwanted background sounds, such as the ticking of a clock. You can do fine editing of this kind in your DAW, but sometimes it's more efficient to clean up your files with a waveform editor first, before importing them into your DAW. *TwistedWave* is a straightforward and reliable waveform editor app.

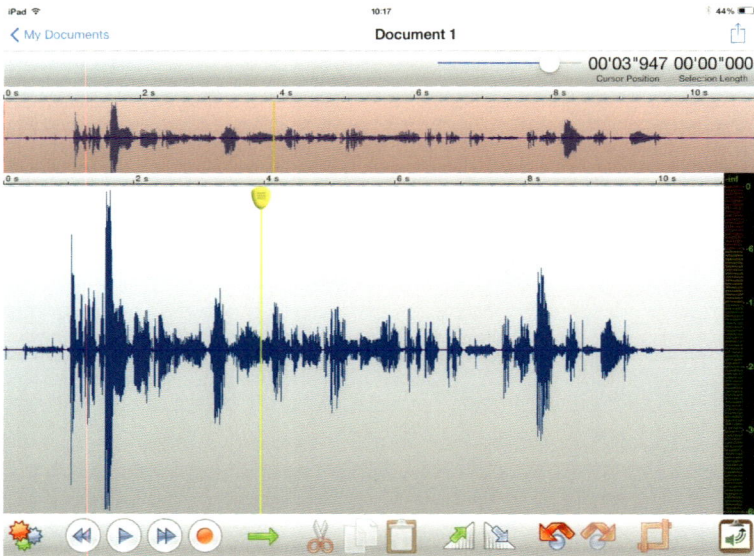

TwistedWave

There's quite a choice of reputable brand-name DAW apps, though many of them are geared more to MIDI tracks rather than to audio. Streets ahead of the competition is *Auria* - though it carries a hefty price tag for an app (around £35). For that, though, you get up to 24 recording tracks and 48 playback channels of 64 bit/96kHz digital audio, plus a comprehensive range of processing and effects, including convolution reverb*, plus (as an in-app additional purchase) the facility to import video into a playback window, synchronised to the audio. Note, though, that there's no MIDI, so if you want to compose MIDI sounds or music, you'll have to do it in a MIDI app like *Music Studio* or *GarageBand* and bounce it down to an audio track for import into Auria.

* a type of reverb processing based on mathematical calculations of the acoustic characteristics of real spaces.

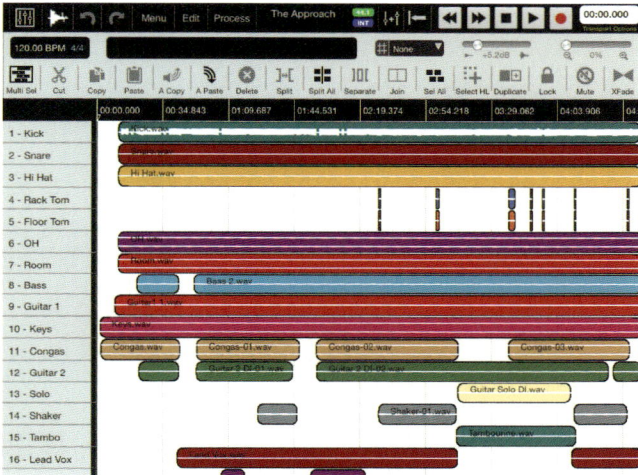

Auria (timeline screen)

Auria (mixer screen)

If your sound design needs aren't that complex and you're just looking for an app that's straightforward to use and provides the basic set of audio processing tools (EQ, compression, reverb and delay), then *MultiTrack DAW* fits the bill at a fifth of the price of Auria.

You don't need anything else to construct a perfectly acceptable drama, documentary, TV commercial, or film trailer; and it might actually be quite refreshing to work with just these tools on a music video or animation project. Too many student projects are spoiled by over-indulgence in digital effects, which all too quickly become annoying clichés - a poor substitute for real creativity.

Not on the iPad

On the other hand, you may prefer at this point to say "thanks, but no thanks" to your iPad. Post-production is where the limitations of the iPad really start to show, especially in comparison to what high-end software is capable of these days. If you have access to a video editing suite at your college, then this is the time to export everything off your iPad. Even a good laptop computer such as an Apple MacBook Pro will be a huge step up from an iPad, especially if it has software such as Final Cut and Logic Studio installed.

Video editing on desktop computers is, though, outside the scope of this book; so while the next section is equally applicable to desktop editing, I have limited it to what is achievable on the iPad alone.

The editing process: rough cuts and fine cuts

You should, if your production assistants did their job properly on location, have all your footage, together with log sheets indicating which takes are useable and which not. Your first task is to trim your clips as you want them (though still retaining the clapperboard ID's if you recorded sound separately) and drag them to the timeline. At this stage, you should just butt clips together: don't bother with any transitions. Also, try not to get distracted by issues of detail: now is not the time to get everything perfect. At this stage, concentrate on the wood, not the trees.

Once you have everything you want on the timeline, it is good practice to complete an *edit decision list* - a paper record of your timeline, showing in and out points for your clips, together with comments to be addressed at the fine editing stage. In some ways this is a hangover from the days of tape-based analogue editing: the only way you could prepare editing instructions then was with a piece of paper showing precise in-points and out-points in time-code for each clip. However, it's still a very useful thing to do: it provides you with an easy way of splitting up the work between you, and making a record of who is to edit which sections; it thus also provides evidence for the assessor as to who did what; and it's a handy aide-memoire, should you accidentally forget to save your work, and have to re-do a section.

Meanwhile, if you recorded sound separately, you should also be working on your soundtrack clips, balancing and sweetening the dialogue. You should then insert them onto the dialogue track in sync with the video. You can now safely trim your clapperboard ID's off your clips.

Now you have everything assembled in the right order, it's time to go through it in detail, first sequence by sequence, then scene by scene. Concentrate this time on creating a sense of rhythm, pace, and emotional impact. Trim shots to make sequences work - so that a cutaway is not too long, for instance. If a sequence doesn't seem to work as you had hoped, forget your storyboard and experiment a little. Maybe the cutaway would work better *after* the reaction shot, rather than before? Try it. Insert your transitions, also, at this point.

When you are happy with your sequences, re-visit your soundtrack and insert any pre-recorded wildtrack or spot effects you want to use on an effects track, together with any Foley effects. Finally, add background music, if you are using it, onto a third, music track.

You now have a completed rough-cut, and it might be a good idea to do a test screening to a carefully-chosen audience before proceeding further. Get some reaction from people who haven't been too close to it, as you will inevitably be by now.

If your video has to be of a specified duration (a TV commercials assignment, for example, might have a time-constraint in seconds, or your drama might have to fit a five-minute slot), then you will probably have to do some more editing for time. If your rough-cut is too long, this may just require some creative compromises. Audience reaction from a test screening may well be helpful in assisting you to cut in the right places. If, on the other hand, it is too short and you don't have any more material, then you have a real problem…

When - and only when - you have your essential content in complete and final form, you can move on to the fine cut. It is at this stage that you:

> • Run sequences through a grading app if you need to, to do any colour corrections for continuity that may be needed, or apply a tint, or turn off the saturation if you want black-and-white;

• Work on your title sequences, credits, and any other sections that require text or graphics;

• Do any final balancing or sweetening of your soundtracks.

The very last stage is to export your completed master file, so that, at the very least, each of you has (or has online access to) a copy, and your assessors can view it. Probably, you will want to go beyond this to some form of public distribution. Both iMovie and Pinnacle Studio offer a choice of export options, from simple emailing (better with Dropbox or Hightail for large files) to compression and uploading to sites such as YouTube, Facebook, and Vimeo. You can also share your file with a desktop PC via iCloud. Note, though, that - depending on the desktop equipment and generation of software you are using - you may have some difficulties in burning a DVD. Online distribution is generally a lot more straightforward than DVD creation.

7: The film trailer

Trailers are montages. They do not have a linear narrative. Their purpose is to whet the appetite by indicating (i) the genre, and (ii) the pleasures offered by the film. They are compilations of ingredients; not in the order they come in the film, but montaged together in a way which will entice, and stimulate desire to see the film.

They therefore select key aspects - key moments from the film (though not revealing anything set up as a mystery). These key moments typically consist of: *action moments*, *romantic moments*, *comedy moments*, and *the setting up of a mystery or dilemma.* Clips of dialogue are interwoven with voiceover narration that gives just sufficient summary of the plot to set up genre expectations, together with emphasis upon star names (possibly cross-referencing to other films they have starred in). The trailer is functioning, therefore, in exactly the same way as the film poster.

If you have iMovie on your iPad, you will have noticed that it offers an instant trailer making facility. It basically consists of a number of templates for standard Hollywood feature film genres, into which you insert your footage. It is, in other words, a set of well-worn old trailer clichés.

You should not - *repeat not* - use these for your coursework assignments. They are, however, worth having a look at, and maybe even formally analysing, since they do usefully point up the differences in approach used for different genres of film to attract their target audiences. They're a useful starting point for thinking about your own.

8: The music video

The music video was originally invented as a way of promoting the song on the soundtrack. In recent years, though, it has increasingly come to be seen as a form of the product in its own right, rather than just as merchandising. Many music fans prefer to watch songs being performed on MTV or YouTube, rather than just listen to them on their MP3 player or stereo.

The music video is a highly creative form of video production, responsible for many innovations in style and technique. Music video products are so varied that it is difficult to pin down 'the essential characteristics of the form'. However, the following principles generally apply:

• There is nothing on the soundtrack other than the song.

• The visual content, however, is limited only by your imagination. Like the fashion industry, anything goes, so long as it stands out from the crowd.

• There are two basic approaches: the performance video, and the narrative video. A common variation is to combine the two. The performance video shows the singer or band performing the song. The narrative video is a storyline with characters (who may or may not be members of the band), who act out a situation related to the lyrics of the song.

• The visual content must be appropriate to the song; the two must meld happily together. At its simplest, in the narrative video the visual content will directly illustrate the lyric: *show* the same story that the words *tell*, so that the whole becomes like a single song clip from a film musical. Alternatively, a generalised lyric, or the overall mood of the song, may inspire a storyline which takes the song in a whole new direction.*

* one of the most impressive pieces of student work I have seen was based on a song which was, in a very general way, about feelings of loneliness and isolation. The video which they made was a 'day in the life' of a homeless person, showing him begging, mooching aimlessly around the park, and so on. What began as simply a rather sad song became suddenly very powerful.

The choice of approach will usually be determined by the music genre of the song and its target audience. Romantic pop songs aimed at pre-teen girls, for example, are more likely to have narrative videos than genres such as rap, which will usually be aimed at an older, more male, audience.

Music genres, as they develop, tend to become associated with particular styles of video. A successful, innovative, video may be imitated by other bands playing similar kinds of music, in order to attract the same audience. The visual style thus often morphs into a genre in its own right.

An important function of the music video is to establish or reinforce the 'branding' of the artists: what it is about them that gives them their particular unique appeal, their 'brand image'. This may be already well established, or it may be something not yet fully developed. Either way, it should be your prime focus in discussing ideas for videos with singers/bands and their managements.

The 'indie' video relates to the 'commercial' video rather in the way that independent film contrasts with mainstream cinema: the indie product has a more low-budget feel, a more up-market and discerning feel, more original, more subtle, more interesting - but more niche. The commercial product feels more like a glitzy, showbizzy, mass-produced factory product giving a majority audience more of the same, rather than something new.

Like much product aimed at young people, music videos often play with themes of transgression and rebellion. There are, however, ethical boundaries which must be respected. The visual content should not be inappropriate to the likely target audience of the artist and song. It should not, for example, cross accepted boundaries of taste and decency. A pop video aimed at young teens or pre-teens may contain mild erotic content such as skimpy dress, but must not be based on themes such as violence or sado-masochism.

9: The drama

For the purposes of this section, I am including under the general umbrella of 'drama' all forms of video product that are scripted fictional stories: film genres (such as action-adventure, rom-com etc); art films; television soaps, situation comedies, drama genres (such as the police procedural); and so on.

To stand any chance of being awarded Distinction, your work must move beyond acceptably competent (Pass), and beyond highly competent (Merit) to impressively creative. A drama project should therefore aim at originality and creativity. Warmed-over imitations of familiar fare won't cut it. However well it is made, it will fall short of the criteria for Distinction.

When considering ideas for a drama project, therefore, you would be wise to reject from the start ideas which your assessors greet with a groan of "Oh no, not another one!" You can bet that high on most "spare me!" lists will be:

- *Anything* involving zombies;

- Horror (and comedy-horror);

- Slasher (and comedy-slasher);

- Low-life/gangland confrontations in multi-storey car parks;

- Stories about bullying set mainly in school toilets;

- Hollyoaks-type scenarios.

If you really want to do one of these, then it has to be really special, and work extra hard not to be seen as derivative (remember that word: *derivative*. The kiss of death to hopes of Distinction).

Getting ideas

Drama is conflict

All good dramatic stories are based on a conflict of some kind. Without conflict, there's nowhere for a story to go. There are many kinds of conflict, but they can be usefully collected together into four broad areas:

- Internal conflict: fighting my demons - *The Truman Show, Chariots of Fire.*

- Interpersonal conflict: clashes with other individuals - *Matilda, Dirty Harry.*

- Social/institutional conflict: the individual against the organisation or wider society -   *Nineteen Eighty-Four, The Elephant Man, Dead Poets' Society.*

- Conflict with the non-human world: natural forces, the wild - *Jaws, Scott of the Antarctic, Jurassic Park.*

So when you are tossing initial ideas around in your group, try to identify where the key areas of conflict are. If there isn't one, then you don't yet have a story. If you're stuck, try putting two ideas together, and seeing what happens when they collide. For example:

- a man goes for an evening stroll *(not yet a story).*

- a totalitarian government forbids citizens to leave their homes at night *(not yet a story).*

Put the two together, though, and have a police car pass by, and you have a story (Ray Bradbury's *The Pedestrian*).

There are only 7 stories in the world...

Christopher Booker, in his book *The 7 Basic Plots*, claims that most stories, in the way they unfold and develop, can be seen as variations upon a relatively small number of archetypal narratives. These are:

- Overcoming the monster - *Jaws, Frankenstein.*

- Rags to riches - *Cinderella, Pretty Woman.*

- The quest - *Lord of the Rings, Indiana Jones.*

- Voyage and return - *Alice in Wonderland, Around the World in Eighty Days.*

- Comedy (in its Ancient Greek sense: initial confusion being resolved with a happy ending) - *Tootsie, Notting Hill.*

- Tragedy (meaning a downward spiral to a doomed ending) - *Lolita, Dr Jekyll and Mr Hyde.*

- Rebirth - *A Christmas Carol, Beauty and the Beast.*

Others have suggested different kinds of archetype, such as:

- The chase - *The Matrix, The 39 Steps.*

- The bonds of friendship - *Butch Cassidy and the Sundance Kid, Thelma and Louise.*

- The superhero saves the day - *James Bond films, spaghetti westerns.*

- The triumph of the underdog - *Forrest Gump, Little Voice.*

No doubt you can think of others yourself. The point, though, is that there are tried and tested narrative structures to stories. If you recognise that an initial idea might fit into one of these kinds of category, then you have a way forward for story development that you can be confident will work.

Planning and script development

Writing is rewriting. Your first draft of a script is bound to be a bit of a mess. The job of the first draft is to turn nothing into something. Once you have that something, you can start polishing it and giving it some shape. Here's how:

- Try to tell the story through the action and through what we see, more than through the dialogue. Most first drafts are far too wordy, too dependent on dialogue for carrying the story forward. Engage us through action and emotion, not through information.

- Keep dialogue to the minimum you can get away with, and - unless you are doing Shakespeare - natural and conversational. We don't normally speak in long, complex sentences, so don't write them.

- Establish characters through mise-en-scéne, costume and by the way they behave, rather than through dialogue or explanation, as much as you can.

With the exception of television soap operas, most dramas (including parallel narratives) fall into three parts: beginning, middle, and end; with the middle section taking the lion's share of screen time. In the world of screenplay writing these are known as *set-up*, *confrontation*, and *resolution*. Together, they form the *three-act structure*. Syd Field's classic guides to screenplay writing advise that Act I and Act III should each take up about a quarter of the screen time, with Act II taking the remaining two quarters. The movement from one Act to another is achieved with a *plot point*. For example, following the initial introduction to the characters and situation in Act I, Act II might begin at the point when the hero embarks on the job that is to be done. Act II might end when a crucial fact is finally revealed, leading to the consequences in Act III. It's a good idea to hammer your story into this kind of broad shape, if you can.

Budget considerations

Shooting a piece of drama is likely to involve you in *actual* costs, not just pretend ones you make up   when you are learning how to do a budget sheet. You are bound to need props of some kind, and you might need costumes. There may be travel costs in getting to locations. Some locations may involve fees or charges of some kind. Then there's car parking. If you are travelling some distance, then you may need to set aside money for food: while you yourself may be happy to pay out of your own pocket, it's not fair to expect your actors to incur costs. If you pay their expenses and feed them, they'll be happy; if you don't, they may drop out.

This means you must be very practical in estimating how much money you will need, and in working to raise it before you start on your production. You can, of course, put money into the kitty yourselves, and ask around your families for a bit of sponsorship. A better idea, though, is to try to *make* some money, for example by taking part in a sponsored marathon, or getting a local band to do a benefit gig, or running a cake stall, or a car-boot sale, or doing some ebay trading. If your drama has a social action message of some kind, then you might be able to interest a local company or charity in sponsoring it in return for a mention in your credits and on your packaging and publicity - but don't be too hopeful of this. Too many groups spend too much time chasing corporate sponsorship, only to learn the hard way that businesses aren't terribly keen to throw money away if there's not much in it for them.

Don't forget that it's not just the production stage that will cost you money. Research may involve costs: travel, photocopying, guidebooks, maps, and so on. Location recces mean more car parking charges or bus fares, more coffee and sandwiches, possibly an entrance fee to pay.

Location shooting

You'll need your storyboards and your shooting schedule. If sequences are too complicated for storyboard frames to be self-explanatory, then supplement them with a *shot list* - a written instruction for each shot, including in-shot camera movements, dialogue cues, and any other necessary explanation.

If you have time, shoot a few cutaways or reaction shots in addition to what's on your storyboard. They might be useful if you have a continuity problem at the edit.

The sound recordist should also take care to record a few minutes of dialogue-free wildtrack at some point - the background sounds of the location. You may need some to cover an awkward edit (for instance if the sound of an approaching lorry suddenly disappears altogether at a vision cut).

Take your time, and allow sufficient time to pack up and leave in an orderly fashion when you've finished. Never leave a location in a hurry - you're bound to leave something behind. Have a checklist of every item of equipment and prop you take with you, and check them off as you pack up. It's all too easy to overlook small (but precious) items when you're in a hurry.

You should each take sole responsibility for particular items of equipment etc. Don't help each other to pack bags. *Only* the person who knows what should be in the bag should pack it.

Post-production

Cut it all roughly together first, before working on the detail. That way, you get an overview perspective on what you have, and any major problems come to light early on.

Then work on each sequence, checking for continuity errors as you go, and ensuring that match-on-action and shot-reverse-shot sequences are correctly constructed, and that you have not made any 180° rule errors.

Then build sequences into scenes, stretching and squeezing as needful to establish a sense of rhythm and pace.

Then, once you have your scenes knocked more or less into shape, turn your full attention to your soundtrack. Sound is an extremely important element in a drama production. It needs as much care and attention put into it as the pictures. Sadly, all too often, it doesn't get it. Poor sound is probably the most common cause of lost marks in student drama videos. Everyone gets too caught up in the shaping of shots into sequences, sequences into scenes, and post-production effects - and time runs out. Allow sufficient time to do all your mixing, layering and sweetening of your soundtrack. At the end of the day, if time does run out, a few corners cut on the pictures, but with good sound, is much better than having perfect pictures but rough sound.

Finally, apply the lipstick and eyeshadow with your grading app, add your soundtrack music, and prepare your test screening master.

10: The documentary

Of all types of video product, this is the one that will involve the most in-depth and careful work at the pre-production stage, most especially in research. If you are producing factual content, then it is vitally important to get your facts right. In development and content research, use reliable sources and get into the habit of checking and double-checking everything. The internet, particularly, is chock-full of traps for the unwary.

Your starting point may be a particular issue which has caught your attention; or you may simply decide you want to make a documentary, and then have to scratch around for ideas for the subject-matter. Either way, try not to bite off more than you can chew. Subjects like global warming or animal rights are just too big to address in one single small documentary. Keep your subject-matter specific, tight, local, and focused.

Before starting work on your own ideas, you should take time to view a range of existing documentaries. Look at different types of narrative construction: the in-vision reporter, the unseen reporter, the fly-on-the-wall. Ask yourself why different approaches were chosen for different kinds of subject-matter. Why is one approach more suitable than another?

Don't just look at mainstream documentary programmes on television; trawl the internet for more radical documentaries (websites such as Sheffield Doc/Fest http://sheffdocfest.com/ and the International Documentary Association http://www.documentary.org/ are good places to start - or just go to Vimeo and type in "documentaries"). Television documentaries, particularly in the UK, are usually very careful to be neutral and objective, to present the various sides in a debate in a balanced way. The over-riding principle of objectivity and balance is central to the Reithian BBC tradition of public-service broadcasting which has dominated British broadcast journalism from the start. Outside of the mainstream, though, many documentary-makers take a much more polemical approach, presenting impassioned accounts of one side of a debate, in an unashamedly biased way.

There are advantages and disadvantages to this. Polemical documentaries are more rousing and involving, as they are not so concerned about maintaining a careful distance from controversial issues. However, their obvious bias means they may be regarded as lacking authority. We may find them entertaining or inspiring - but we are less inclined to trust them. Reithian documentaries, on the other hand, run the risk of becoming boring, or leaving us confused about the rights and wrongs of complex issues, having been so careful to present them so fairly in all their complexity.

When you come to plan your own documentary, having settled on your subject-matter, the very next thing you should do - before you start on any detailed planning - is to clarify your intended distribution strategy. This is because you need to have a clear understanding of the institutional constraints you may have to work within, and issues of representation that may arise. Without this, you have no solid, practical basis for choosing one approach over another.

If for example, you are intending to make a documentary about a controversial town planning scheme, for broadcast on a local community television station, then you will need to be aware that the station is required to abide by the Ofcom Broadcasting Code. If your documentary infringes the code in, for instance, not exercising due impartiality, or presents prejudiced representations of one side or other in the controversy, then the station is not going to risk losing its licence by broadcasting your programme.

At the production stage, make sure to obtain signed releases from all participants in your documentary. If anyone changes their mind about their agreement to be seen in your programme and you don't have a release from them, you may have to re-edit in order to exclude them.

At the editing stage, be careful that you do not accidentally (and certainly not deliberately!) misrepresent what people say. It is all too easy to suggest, for example, that someone supports something, when they in fact oppose it, if they have discussed the issue at length and you cut out large amounts of what they say.

11: The client brief

Most schools and colleges are keen to make links with local employers, so that they can set up activities such as work experience placements and group visits, and arrange visiting speakers for speech days, citizenship classes, and so on. One other way in which employers often get involved is by sponsoring a project or competition of some kind, such as a student newspaper or fashion show - or a video product.

This is manna from heaven for video tutors keen to introduce their students to real-world production practices. If the media course you are on includes 'working with a client' as one of its categories for production work, then you are going to find yourself having to adapt to a very different way of working from most other assignments: to someone else's specifications, rather than your own.

Employers will, of course, be careful to protect their businesses. They are unlikely to trust you to come up with television commercials for their products, cr corporate public relations materials. The kind of brief they are most likely to come up with will either be an instructional video about one of their products (how to assemble a piece of flat-pack furniture, for example), or a training video to use with their staff (on a new procedure, for instance, or an aspect of health and safety in the workplace).

My students one year were treated to a client brief from the local police station. Their community liaison officer asked them to make two short training videos, one to be called 'How to Steal a Car', and the other to be called 'How to Burgle a House'. Part of his job was to give talks to Neighbourhood Watch groups, and the idea was that these videos would be good discussion starters at these meetings.

The students split into two production teams and took one brief each. Both groups had a thoroughly enjoyable time doing the necessary research, planning and production work. Essentially, their finished videos were 'Crimewatch reconstruction'- type drama shorts, except that the narration scripts did not take the usual tone of shocked disapproval, but instead offered 'helpful advice' to the trainee criminal.

The client was very pleased with them, and I gather they livened up his talks quite considerably…

If, by the way, your brief is about health and safety, you should take extra care to ensure that your demonstrations of carelessness or bad practice do not themselves create actual health and safety hazards. You mustn't ask your actors to fall from scaffolding onto piles of bricks, just to show that it's a bad idea.

12: Distribution: staying legal

You might not have plans to do anything in reality with your video product beyond submitting it for assessment. However, it's likely that you'll still be required to research and prepare a distribution strategy and create marketing materials. This might be for the same assignment brief, or for a linked assignment or unit of work. So long as it all remains hypothetical, and your video doesn't actually get screened anywhere outside your college, then it's not a big issue.

If, however, you are thinking of some form of *actual* public distribution, then legal rights and restrictions will become a major factor affecting every stage of your production. You don't want to get into trouble for infringement of someone's copyright, for example. Here are some issues to which you may have to give serious thought:

> • You mustn't tell people appearing in your film that it is only for college, and then change your mind without consulting them. The MD of your local plant breeding laboratory might be quite happy to grant you an interview for a college documentary assignment, but will be extremely displeased if it ends up going viral on Twitter and his premises are vandalised by anti-GM campaigners. He would be within his rights to seek legal redress.

> • Get all your actors to sign release forms, and give them a copy. You never know: one of them might get a place at drama school - or decide to join the police force - and all of a sudden become unhappy about appearing all over the internet in your film. If you don't have a signed release form, you're scuppered.

> • If you are using actors/contributors under 18, (and especially if you are using actors/contributors under 16) there are a lot of regulations to consider; and you should not do anything without consulting your tutors. You will need to get consent forms signed by parents; you may need to get adults working with them CRB-checked; and you will have to be very careful that the script and other content of your film does

not contain unsuitable subject-matter or language, or place inappropriate requirements upon them. See, for example, the Channel 4 guidelines for film-makers:

http://www.channel4.com/media/documents/commissioning/LEGAL/GuidelinesForWorkingWithUnder18s.pdf

• Get permissions in writing for the use of locations. Make sure you are clear and accurate about your distribution plans. Parents, for example, may be OK about their home being used for a college assignment, but not so happy about their privacy being invaded on YouTube.

• Don't use anyone else's music on your soundtrack unless it's clearly marked 'copyright-free', or you have obtained a licence to use it. Don't take any chances: for instance, a classical piece may be out of copyright as a work, but performers and/or recording companies may still have rights to protect. Similarly, don't use sampling techniques for composing your own music without permission from the copyright owners of the original work. If friends create and perform original music for you as a favour, get them to sign a release form: if your film starts to make serious money, they may regret having done it for you for free, and chase you for a cut of the profits. Without a signed release form, you're in a very weak position if they set their solicitors onto you.

• Obtain copyright clearance, in writing, in advance, on everything that is someone else's intellectual property that you want to include in your film; for example, visual materials such as documents and photographs, or spoken materials such as an extract from a poem, or clips from other films. You will need to be clear and specific about your distribution plans: they will affect the scale of fees being charged - and possibly whether or not permission is granted.

• If you want to adapt an existing work into another form ('Finnegan's Wake - The Musical'), this will take negotiation which you can expect to take some time, and is more likely than not to result in a refusal of permission. It's probably not a good choice, therefore, if you are aiming at public distribution. Keep it in-college, coursework only, and you should be OK.

• Don't assume, just because something is easily downloadable from the internet, that it is in the public domain. It probably isn't.

13: Distribution and marketing strategies

If you are intending to organise actual distribution of your video, and have been allowed to do so, the possibilities depend on its nature and purpose. If, for instance, you are making a campaigning documentary for a cause of some kind, then it makes sense to discuss your project with the relevant charity or social action organisation from the start. They may well commission your video, assist you with funding, and finance the distribution of the video once it is completed. They may, for instance, have it burned professionally to DVD to sell or give away, or perhaps include it on their website.

Similarly, if you are making a promotional video, it make sense to hook up formally with the place or organisation being promoted, and come to a mutually beneficial agreement on funding and distribution. The local tourist board, for example, might sponsor a 'My Town' project.

If you are making a music video for a local band, then they may offer to purchase the rights, so they they can use it as part of their own promotion and merchandising, or to brighten up their website or Facebook page. You get a fee; they get the right to do what they like with your video.

If your video is a drama short, a comedy short, an art film, or a factual feature, you may be thinking of uploading to Vimeo or YouTube. If so, you should consider their differences.

Vimeo operates as a sharing site for independent film-makers. You will certainly get a big audience for your film - but you won't make any money. It's a good site to go to if you simply want your work to be seen by other film-makers, and to network generally with the independent film community.

YouTube, on the other hand, as well as being a sharing site, is now also a serious commercial distribution outlet. It began as a site showing only limited-size clips, but it can now happily handle full length feature films. You can make money by allowing the inclusion of commercials at the start of and within your stream. You get paid for this whenever someone watches your film. If you know what you're doing, it's possible to make substantial amounts of money this way. See, for example, the following blog from an independent film-maker:

http://www.shericandler.com/2013/07/03/releasing-your-feature-film-on-youtube/

If you are intending to take advantage of this opportunity on YouTube, you don't just upload your video as normal: you have to join the YouTube Partner Programme, submit your video, and prove you own all the rights. However, if you succeed, you will start to make income from your work, and you can legitimately call yourself a professional.

14: And finally, your evaluation...

Your individual evaluation is important: in borderline cases, it's often the deciding factor as to whether to award the higher grade. Don't leave it until the last minute. Don't view it as a minor irritation to get done and over with as quickly as possible. Your evaluation is where you reveal the depth and quality of your understanding of what it is you and your group have achieved together. It needs to be reflective, informed, and critical. "I thought it was ace..." won't do.

Your tutors may require a particular way of going about it: if so, do as you're told. If not, here's how it's usually done:

Stage 1

Prepare for it by getting audience feedback following a screening of your finished video. You could do this with questionnaires, focus-group discussions, or a combination of the two. Don't just take questions/comments from the audience - it's likely to be too random, too brief, too difficult to make notes of, and weak in terms of portfolio evidence. If your video is aimed at a particular audience demographic, try to get your audience as representative of that demographic as you can. For example, if your product is aimed at children, the opinions of adults alone won't be enough.

Collect together your feedback findings and write a summary of the main points.

Stage 2

Convene a 'post-mortem' meeting of your group. Everyone must attend. At this meeting, you discuss, at length and in detail, *three* things:

> • Your feelings and thoughts about the strengths and weaknesses of *the product;*

> • Your feelings and thoughts about the strengths and weaknesses of *the production process* (i.e. the way you went about it);

• What the audience feedback reveals - especially where it differs from your own views.

This meeting should <u>not</u> have a minute-taker: each of you should make your own notes, in preparation for Stage 3.

Stage 3

On your own, write your evaluation. This should consist of *three* sections:

• Your own detailed summary of the conclusions of the group post-mortem meeting;

• A section in which you add your own individual comments upon, or disagreements with, the group view;

• Finally, reflect on what you yourself have learned for the future through participation in this project. This might, for instance, be technical skills you have gained, or lessons you have learned about working with others, or comments on "how I would go about it differently next time - and why".

Try in each section of your evaluation to include comments upon both the product, and the production process. Keep them separate, and try to give them reasonably equal weight.

Fin

ABOUT THE AUTHOR

The author has taught and managed Further Education sector Media Studies and Media Production courses for over twenty years. He has also worked as an External Verifier for BTEC Nationals in Media, and is a Visiting Moderator for OCR.